CHRISTIAN LEADERSHIP BLUEPRINT

A PURPOSE-DRIVEN GUIDE TO PERSONAL AND SPIRITUAL TRANSFORMATION

Manifest Your Greatness Now

SHAUNA-KAYE BROWN

Christian Leadership Blueprint
A Purpose-Driven Guide to Personal and Spiritual Transformation

Published by:
Transform Nations Now LLC
Powder Springs, GA
www.shaunakbrownspeaks.com

TRANSFORM NATIONS NOW LLC
Manifest Your Greatness Now

Interior layout and cover design by Transform Nations Now LLC

Ordering Information:
Special discounts are available for quantity purchases by associations, corporations, institutions, and other entities or persons. Please direct your inquiries to shaunakbrownspeaks@gmail.com

ISBN: 979-8-9874038-2-2 (Paperback)
First Edition: 2025
Printed in the United States of America

DEDICATION

To my students, my teachers and those who desire to lead according to God's divine plan. To every servant-hearted believer who has chosen to say *yes* to the call of leadership, not for recognition or applause, but out of obedience to Christ. To those who have felt the weight of responsibility, the cost of sacrifice, and the tension of influence, yet press forward with humility and grace. To those who long to lead like Jesus, with compassion, integrity, wisdom, and truth. May this book be a reminder that your calling is sacred, your labor is not in vain, and your legacy, when rooted in Christ, will echo for generations.

Lead boldly! Lead faithfully! Lead surrendered!

ACKNOWLEDGMENTS

This work is the result of intentional learning and personal development. It is also the collective contribution of my mentors, teachers, family, friends, and trusted advisors. I am conscious of the fact that we are the sum of our experiences, acquired knowledge, and the input of those we encounter. All of this helps to mold us on our journey to realizing our inherent greatness.

I am profoundly grateful to the Holy Spirit, my ever-present companion and unfailing guide. In moments when the path felt unclear or the burden felt heavy, His wisdom steadied me and His presence refreshed me. He breathed life into every page and courage into every pause. Through His strength, I overcame obstacles that threatened to halt the process, and through His peace, I remained steadfast. This work is not merely a reflection of my effort, but a testament to His grace. Without Him, none of this would have been possible.

To Dr. Caswell Morgan, Dean of the New Greater Bethel Bible Institute (NGBBI), for your visionary leadership and unfaltering support during the writing process. Your staunch commitment to academic and spiritual excellence has been a source of continual inspiration and fortitude.

To Dr. Jean Richards, thank you for your guidance and commitment to cultivating both scholarship and character in me. Your feedback, continuous encouragement, and support were invaluable. To my classmates in my Master's program, thank you for your prayers, support, and shared wisdom. Your presence during the journey reminded me that we were never meant to lead alone. I am especially grateful for the community we built, the accountability we shared, and the joy of pressing through together.

A heartfelt thank you to Dr. Errol Brown and Dr. Isabel St. Vil for your invaluable teaching and mentorship during the training classes. Alongside Dr. Morgan, your investment in me as a leader has made a lasting impact. Your instructions challenged me to grow, dig deeper, and lead with greater clarity and conviction. This work is not the product of one mind, but the reflection of many voices, prayers, and spiritual investments. Thank you all for walking this path with me.

To God be all the glory!

"The goal of leadership is not to gain followers but to produce leaders who reflect the heart of God."

—Shauna-kaye Brown

CONTENTS

"True transformation begins when we stop chasing position and start embracing purpose."

—Shauna-kaye Brown

PREFACE

Every book carries a story between its pages. This one did not begin with ambition, but with adversity. But, as James Allen says, "adversity introduces a man to himself." While writing, I found myself in a battle against procrastination, anxiety, and the pressure of navigating a high-stress, emotionally draining season. For a long time, the thought of writing felt overwhelming, a mountain too steep to climb. My initial goal was not to produce something grand, but simply to finish the thesis, submit it, and move on. By the grace of God, I accomplished that and breathed a sigh of relief. Yet, in His providence, God had more in mind than I could have ever envisioned. What you now hold is the fruit of His divine redirection, a work born not out of ease, but out of submission to a promise I could not yet perceive.

This book would not exist without the unwavering voice and vision of Dr. Caswell Morgan, Dean of the New Greater Bethel Bible Institute. He consistently challenged me and every student under his care, to believe beyond the immediate expectation of an assigned thesis. "Your thesis can become a book," he would often declare. At the time, the possibility seemed far-fetched, noble, perhaps. But far removed from the anxiety-laced reality I lived in. Yet Dr.

Morgan's words lingered ceaselessly throughout the writing process. A few weeks after submitting the original assignment, his voice returned to my consciousness. "Many go on to turn their theses into books." The words stirred something dormant within me, and with time, I began to discern that this was not just an echo of a professor's encouragement. It was the prompting of the Holy Spirit. Despite the voices in my head that insisted it could not be done, there was one distinct voice in the reservoir of my heart that gently prodded me into a paradoxical reality. I was impelled to choose which voice I would incline to. It was not an easy choice as I was constantly plagued with discouragement and needless distractions, but God had a plan that remained unfaltering.

Christian Leadership Blueprint is the outcome of saying 'yes' to God, particularly in the moments when obedience felt most difficult. As you can see, it was not birthed in convenience or comfort. Every chapter reflects a study of leadership as well as a journey through my own transformation as a leader, devotee, intercessor, and servant of Christ. In truth, what you now hold in your hands is somewhat a memorial. A demonstration of how God takes what feels like fragments and weaves them into something whole. It is a call to Kingdom leaders across the nations of this world who sense the weight of the mantle but wonder if they can carry it. The answer is a resounding yes, but not in your strength, in case you were inclined to harbor doubt, but in God's.

The Apostle Paul reminds us in 2 Corinthians 12:9, "My grace is sufficient for thee: for my strength is made perfect in weakness." This verse underscores the truth that Kingdom leadership does not require perfection. It requires surrender. In writing the original thesis, I found strength to persevere only after intentionally surrendering everything to God. Paul's journey teaches us that spiritual authority often emerges through personal weakness, because that is where the power of God rests most fully. That has been my experience. And I pray that as you journey through these pages, it becomes yours as well. Whatever has immobilized you, may you come to know it so you can intentionally, purposefully, and completely surrender.

THE THINKING THAT SETS LEADERS APART

What separates effective leaders from those who merely manipulate through fear, flattery, and force? The answer lies in their thinking. This is the missing element that distinguishes positional leaders from purposeful difference-makers who plan on creating meaningful legacy. Positional leaders demand compliance through status and connection with the 'boss'. Purposeful leaders inspire movement through conviction and integrity. The former leads from title. The latter leads from trust. **Effective leaders cultivate a distinct mindset shaped by a deep journey of self-discovery.** This inner work produces a positive outlook and a confident belief in their capacity to drive meaningful transformation in the world around them.

This book was written to cultivate the kind of thinking that reflects the mind of Christ; selfless, sacrificial, Spirit-led, and strategic. Philippians 2:5-7 compels us with the words, "Let this mind be in you, which was also in Christ Jesus: Who, being in the form of God, thought it not robbery to be equal with God: But made himself of no reputation, and took upon him the form of a servant." This is the thinking that defines transformational leadership, serving others from divine assignment rather than being led by one's ego. Christ, though possessing all authority, did not grasp for glory. He chose humility. He chose people and that is what authentic leaders do.

THE SERVANT'S MIND

Servant-minded thinking dismantles the cycles of control, people-pleasing, and performance-driven leadership. It liberates leaders from the need for constant validation and cements them instead in divine vision. Leaders who adopt this mindset do not lead through manipulation nor insecurity. They lead through authenticity, grace, and moral conviction to align with purpose. They multiply strength in others rather than seeking to dominate. I once had a manager who would share leadership quotes from executive leaders like John Maxwell and then proceed to express how much he was the embodiment of whatever that quote said. The problem was, the majority of his executive team did not believe this but was too afraid to tell him so instead they would often scramble for ways to boost his ego. I did not dare share my observations with him as he would openly chastise anyone who he thought to be dissenting or of a different opinion. This was a true travesty as I watched someone God wanted to use for His glory sink deeper and deeper in the trap of external validation and self-righteousness. Great leaders cultivate purpose, character, and trust; qualities that not only uplift those they serve but also outlast their own leadership.

Every human being is born with the inherent capacity to lead in the area of their God-given abilities or gifting. Yet very few will invest in honing that capacity. Many will settle for survival, submission to the status quo, or dependence on human approval. But this was never God's design. **You were not created to be a pawn in someone else's power play or to live under perpetual oppression.** You were created to reflect the leadership nature of your Creator. But as long as you allow someone else to determine how you show up, you will remain incapacitated, and that is unfortunate.

Genesis 1:26 reveals this truth: "Let us make man in our image, after our likeness: and let them have dominion..." This is not a cultural suggestion. It is a divine decree. You were made for dominion, not domination over others, but spiritual authority in your sphere of purpose. That means God created you to lead, to create, and to cultivate. To carry influence with character. This book was written to help you reclaim that truth, irrespective of what you were made to believe until now. Nothing is worth your being inauthentic and a mere shadow of your capacity. You are a light and you must do what lights are best known for. You must shine!

May these pages stir something eternal in you. May they confront small thinking and awaken bold faith. May they call you out of fear-based survival and into legacy-driven leadership. And **may you rediscover the mantle God has placed upon your life, not for applause, but for assignment.** You were born to manifest God's greatness in your life.

Now is the time to walk in your calling!

INTRODUCTION

Followers grant the honor of leadership to those they consider worthy of it.

The belief that leadership is an innate trait rather than a developed skill is a grave misconception. While some individuals may be born with natural abilities, Christian leadership is not based solely on inherent skills, charisma, or personality. Instead, it is the product of intentional spiritual foundation, personal discipline, and a heart aligned with the teachings of Jesus Christ encapsulated in His word. When you find yourself out of alignment, you also have to contend with the inevitable challenges that will ensue. This is the reason some people struggle to influence others even though they may have a leadership title or position. Society continues to struggle in various spheres because we lack authentic leadership in churches, educational institutions, corporate businesses, the nonprofit industry, government and a host of other areas.

Leadership can be construed as an enigma whereby those who manage to claim the title often make the mistake of believing they embody it. I invite you to walk with me as we examine the distinctive nature of Christian leadership, rooted not in status or worldly influence, but in servanthood, character development, and intentional spiritual fortitude. These values are not optional qualities, but fundamental pillars that shape the identity and effectiveness of a leader. In Matthew 20:26-28, Jesus reminds us that we find true excellence in service. Anyone Desiring to attain greatness must first learn the intricacies of serving others well.

Many claim the title of servant leader, yet their lives reflect little evidence of genuine service or availability to others.

We live in a time when many claim the title of servant leader, yet their lives reflect little evidence of genuine service or availability to others. Unlike secular leadership models that often emphasize power, prestige and performance, Christian leadership embodies the attributes of Jesus, the 'Good Shepherd,' who exemplifies servanthood and unconditional love. Christian individuals who are serious about their leadership would do well to extensively study His life. Jesus' life and ministry exemplify a leadership style that transforms others into agents of positive change. The primary goal of this study is to present a practical and biblical framework for effective leadership in the church and the broader society, grounded in God's Word and lived through intentionality and deliberate action. It is not enough that we want others to listen to us, we must also recognize the power we have in our hands and begin to lead with purpose.

One of the most significant points of departure between Christian and secular leadership models is that in the latter context, we often perceive popularity, social status, and financial resources as essential prerequisites for leadership. Conversely, meekness and grace as depicted by Jesus in his earthly ministry are primary preconditions for effective Christian leadership. Anyone who desires to lead efficiently must purposely foster and harness these qualities.

DO TRUE SERVANT LEADERS STILL EXIST?

In a world where leadership ideologies and approaches are constantly evolving, Christian leadership remains embedded in principles that transcend societal trends. In this book you will find insights governing how leaders can create transformative influence while remaining grounded in their faith. John Maxwell in his book 'Leader Shift' underscores the importance of a leader's adaptability in an ever-changing environment. He contends that leaders who refuse to make that shift by remaining steadfast to the past find themselves immobilized.

In this context, it reflects a leader's need to be open to change and growth, especially growth into servant leadership. Where Christian leaders are concerned, such growth remains anchored in the immutable foundation of God's Word and fundamental Christian ethics. When your aim is to wave people in the right direction, the Word of God is the only wand you need. The primary objective here is to equip future leaders to embody the teachings of Jesus Christ in all their leadership capacities. This objective finds common ground with Maxwell's purview that indeed the most effective way for a person to honor their calling is to be active in the lives of the people they lead and the world in which they exist. This is in direct alignment with the Christian call to lead with a heart posture of servanthood. Also, to create a positive impact in the lives of others through empathetic and value-driven leadership.

Matthew 5:14-16 reminds us that we are the light of the world and urges us to allow our light to shine for others to see. Through this obedience to doing good work, believers create the space to give glory to God. This scripture highlights the visible impact of a Christian leader's influence and reinforces its intended purpose.

That is, to lead others towards the light of God. By taking a deep dive into Christian principles as the central part of effective leadership, readers are provided with a roadmap.

This roadmap is designed to help them reflect Christ's teaching in different facets of their lives such as decision making, interpersonal relationships, and their overall life mission. Dr. Demetrius Robinson states that, "the key of wisdom is given to those who are called to rule and those that have been designated king."[1] Ultimately, those with the God-given key of wisdom are poised to inspire others to walk in their calling with integrity, accountability, and a steadfast commitment to service. This is the only leadership that counts. Anything else is counterfeit and only exist in the service of self. I know you are able but, this begs the question, are you willing and ready to lead in the service of others?

Fundamentally, Christian leadership is rooted in the Bible. The journey begins by exploring the core principles and traits of an effective leader. This includes defining leadership from a biblical perspective, examining the moral compass of a godly leader, and understanding the precise denotation of identity in Christ. These themes create the foundation for the Christian leader's purpose and influence. Together they make up the Christian Leadership Blueprint. The first chapter lays the foundation for the entire book. It is geared towards helping readers understand that Christian leadership starts with inner transformation that protrudes outward in our actions. True leadership is developed, not inherited. This quickly dispels the false notion that, "leaders are born and not made." Even with intrinsic abilities, becoming the leader God has called you to be requires first an answer to that call and then intentional actions of obedience afterwards.

> *Christian leadership starts with inner transformation that protrudes outward.*

Chapter two explores the development of leadership and contextualizes it as a lifelong journey rather than a sprint. It unpacks the disciplines and developmental processes necessary to become the leader God designed you to be. It includes the role of accountability, character formation and humility. As John Maxwell affirms in several of his works, leadership is a journey, and no one reaches their potential alone.

Christian leaders must embrace continual growth, learning from those who have walked the path before them and accepting support when it is afforded. The more you grow in alignment with the will of God, the process of character development becomes pivotal, shaping both your decisions and how they inspire and impact others. This offers a seamless segue into one of the intricacies of effective Christian leadership that is often overlooked, the role of wisdom.

Chapter three examines what it means to lead from a place that embodies godly wisdom. I submit that wisdom as a general notion is indispensable to leadership. It provides discernment in complex situations, helps manage emotional dynamics, and guides decisions that impact organizations, communities and congregations. Here, we dive into the biblical foundations of wisdom, emotional intelligence, discernment, and vision. You will learn that godly leadership requires more than knowledge; it demands spiritual insight and alignment with the Holy Spirit.

A great depiction of servant leadership is found in John 13:14-15 where Jesus washed his disciples' feet. This experience solidifies the fact that leadership is not so much about dominance but is more concerned with lifting or elevating others. In Jesus one finds a leader who embodies servanthood, steering his followers with purpose and clarity towards the kingdom of God. Here, we must consider how leaders are called to serve, nurture, and uplift those they lead. Jesus led with love even to the extent of laying down his life for us even when we did not deserve it. From this model, Christian leaders in modern society are invited to reflect the same degree of purpose, selflessness, and commitment. This will serve to establish a standard that aligns actions with faith and spiritual accountability. The primary objective is to awaken leaders to the unique assignment God has for each believer who answers the call of leadership. A call that often comes with pain and aloneness.

HARD DOES NOT MEAN IMPOSSIBLE

As much as change is constant, adversity is inevitable. It is therefore imperative that you learn how to lead through crises with a readiness to adapt and resounding faith to withstand the tests time. If I had allowed the difficulty I faced during the research and writing process to deter me, you would not have this divinely orchestrated work in your hands. Working through challenges is especially necessary in the areas of ministry and any other service capacity where people are constantly seeking guidance, direction, hope, and stability. Never forget that someone else's destiny is directly correlated to your fulfilling your purpose. That encompasses your being a purposeful leader. You must find a way to do the hard work unmotivated. In other words, whether or not you act cannot be based solely on how motivated you feel.

Effective crisis leadership requires robust spiritual resilience coupled with practical solutions to help others navigate tough times. In his book by the same name, Robert H. Schuller postulates that, "tough times never last, but tough people do!"[2] An individual's capacity to endure any form of hardship is a testament to their inner strength and ability to persevere beyond the challenging times. It may be difficult but with the right attitude of mind and mission driven by purpose, you will succeed in your bid to impact others.

> *Effective leaders must be equipped to navigate uncertainty with faith, strategy, and resilience.*

Schuler invites readers to allow their hopes instead of their pains and negative experiences to shape their future. This will help believers remain grounded in faith while employing strategic thinking and applying their biblical knowledge to help navigate difficulties. Essentially, we can avoid change as much as we can avert the next challenge. The verdict: a virtual impossibility. Effective leaders must be equipped to navigate uncertainty with faith, strategy, and resilience. Throughout this book, I provide you with strategies for leading effectively in challenging times, handling criticism with grace, and maintaining emotional regulation amidst the inevitable pressures. Strength surfaces when you learn to lean into God's wisdom especially in times of hardship.

Leadership in general comes with many temptations and enticements which can be detrimental to one's salvation. Once a person remains grounded in the ultimate purpose of their divine assignment, they are better equipped to navigate the traps and pitfalls that come with leadership. Power, pride, fame, and isolation are among them and many leaders suffer grave spiritual death because of one or more of these nefarious fiends. This section of the Blueprint dealing with the navigation of traps and pitfalls serves as both a warning and a guide, helping leaders to identify and overcome the snares that have led many to moral failure. It underscores the importance of faithful support systems, accountability, and spiritual grounding. I am not talking about the kind of support that is self-serving and 'fair weather'. I mean those who are not afraid of leading you in the path of righteousness when they see you veering off course.

In traversing the path from the foundation of Christian leadership to the final section of the book, you will see that leaving a legacy that continues to create impact is paramount. It is a defining mark of Christian leadership and extends beyond a leader's natural life. This ideology is grounded in biblical knowledge as seen in Proverbs 13:22. Here, believers are told that a good man's wealth transcends life to leave an inheritance to even his grandchildren. This is more than material wealth, but encompass spiritual wealth, knowledge, and fundamental Christian values that will set you apart. From the scripture, we gather that a leader's influence should form a ripple through generations thus shaping the lives and faith of those to come. Christian Leadership Blueprint also reinforces the significance of mentorship and a commitment to nurturing future leaders. This is a believer's responsibility to the human race. Legacy is not just what we leave behind, but 'who' we leave behind. **A leader's final assignment is to finish well and pass the baton to the next generation with integrity and purpose.**

IT IS NOT ABOUT YOU

I have long understood that the assignment I was placed on this earth to fulfill is not about me. To neglect it would not only dishonor my purpose but fail those whose growth depends on my obedience. When I initially set out to share this journey with the world, I was driven by a deep desire to see Christian leaders rise with boldness to reflect Christ in every sphere of influence. Whether you are at work in the corporate office or at the convenience store grabbing a few essentials, you should endeavor to lead even yourself well. I seek to advance theological understanding while equipping leaders to serve with excellence and authenticity. By examining the essential principles of Christian leadership, this book offers a meaningful contribution to theological scholarship, strengthens leadership development within the Church, and enriches broader conversations on leadership in both faith-based and secular environments.

> *I have long understood that the assignment I was placed on this earth to fulfill is not about me.*

We live in a time that demands more than competence, this season of your life requires a personal conviction to be and to do better. Through this work, I hope to encourage and equip present and future leaders to embody the life and teachings of Jesus Christ, to lead with integrity, and to ignite transformation in their personal life and communities. Everyone has greatness within them, and those who walk in alignment with God's purpose are called to awaken that greatness in others. Christian leadership is, ultimately, a life of service, marked not by titles, but by lives changed and here I present you with the **Christian Leadership Blueprint** to help you do that.

PART ONE:

THE INNER LIFE OF A LEADER

*"The greatest leaders are those
who kneel first."*

—Inspired by Matthew 20:26

CHAPTER 1

THE FOUNDATIONS OF LEADERSHIP

Examining the Core of Leadership

"Leadership is the capacity to translate vision into reality."

— Warren Bennis

Bennis, an established organization expert and pioneer of modern leadership principles, has done extensive work in leadership studies. In his purview, leadership is not simply about having a title or holding authority. Rather, it is about embodying the ability to take something unseen, like an idea or a conviction and bringing it to life in tangible ways that impact others. This kind of leadership demands clarity of purpose, deep character, and the willingness to be shaped by the vision before trying to shape others with it.

In the Kingdom context, vision comes from God. The leader's role is to discern that vision, surrender to it, and then allow God to develop them into someone who can steward it faithfully. Leadership, then, is not self-expression, it is divine obedience. And without the capacity to internalize and live out that vision first, a leader cannot expect others to follow.

Leadership is one of the most spoken about concepts across cultures and contexts, yet in the Kingdom of God, it carries a sacred weight far beyond positions and platforms. At its core it is about influence, but not the kind built on charisma or command. It is influence shaped by conviction, character, and calling. **Before a leader can ever effectively direct others, they must be willing to look inward and examine what truly drives their leadership**:

    A. Is it ambition or assignment?

    B. Is it pride or purpose?

    C. Is it recognition or revelation?

I am inviting you into that introspective space. I encourage you to move past the surface-level strategies and examine the 'heart' of what it means to lead well. Together, let us explore the biblical blueprint for godly leadership, understanding that true leadership is not built overnight, and it certainly is not sustained by gifting alone.

It does not matter how talented you believe yourself to be, or how much praise you receive from people who lack sincerity. Gifting may open doors, but it is character that keeps them open. In this chapter, you will discover the foundational principles that govern effective leadership in the Kingdom and in your everyday life. It is more than worldly wisdom; it is rooted in spiritual truth. Examining the core is where the journey begins.

Leadership Defined

Leadership is often perceived through the lens of influence, authority, or even charisma. In many secular contexts, it is associated with an individual's ability to command, direct, or achieve success through strategic planning and organizational skills. When I served as an executive in leadership, strategic planning, delegation, supervision, and accountability featured often in everyday conversations with other executives and even subordinates. However, while these traits may contribute to effective organizational leadership, the Christian perspective defines leadership on entirely different terms.

When honed and applied with integrity, these attributes can elevate leadership in any sphere. The problem arises when individuals in positions of influence use them in speech but fail to embody them in practice. This creates a paradox that confuses those looking to them for guidance. It becomes a dangerous recipe; an illusion served to the unsuspecting. Be cautious not to fall into the trap of blindly following those whose acclaim rests solely on empty rhetoric.

At its very core, Christian leadership embodies divine calling and responsibility rather than self-appointment. The focus should never be on personal ambition or self-aggrandizement but rather on seeking to aid in fulfilling God's purpose in the lives of others. This is a notable distinction as indicated by John Maxwell in his book 'The 21 Irrefutable Laws of Leadership', where he states that leadership is concerned with influence, nothing more or less. From a Christian worldview, this influence is not just a tool for success, but a sacred trust, meant to reflect Christ's love, wisdom, and character in action. But how often do individuals consider embodying the character of Christ when they are operating in a leadership capacity? Most people become so consumed with impressing and amazing those they lead; they seldom remember to model Christ in the execution of their responsibilities.

Yet, if we were to take a moment to sincerely appreciate the importance of this approach, we would be that much more impactful and influential. Dr. Myles Munroe echoes these sentiments by affirming that, "the essence of leadership is the exercise of influence."[3] Leadership is therefore defined by how a person impacts or guides others, not just by position or title. In fact, the very command that Christ gave to the Christian church in Matthew 28:19-20, is to go into the world and create disciples of everywhere and to teach everything that He has taught us. This is the embodiment of spreading your leadership wings to influence others.

If the Church is to faithfully teach what we have learned from Jesus Christ, then it follows that there exists a clear and inescapable mandate to provide the nations of the world with principled, Christ-centered leadership. Since the year 2022, I have had the privilege of operating my personal growth company 'Transform Nations Now LLC,' a company founded with the express purpose of cultivating positive transformation by teaching individuals across the globe how to live and lead in alignment with God's divine design. To operate effectively within my God-ordained sphere of influence, I am obliged to lead in the manner exemplified by Jesus Christ, that is, with grace, unapologetic truth, and love.

From the unmistakable command articulated in the Great Commission (Matthew 28:19-20), it is evident that the responsibility to develop and deploy effective leaders lies squarely with the Christian Church. And yet, the Church continues to face significant challenges in its capacity to identify, form, and release such leaders. Why is that? It may well be because we have relegated the church to a location rather than realizing it is we who make up the heart of this establishment. Simply put, we are the church!

Why does this leadership gap persist? Many who seek positions of authority within the Church have not taken the necessary time to study the leadership model of Jesus Christ, how He led, and how He continues to lead through the authority of His Word. Until the Church returns to a Christocentric understanding of leadership, informed by Scripture and modeled through discipleship, it will struggle to fulfill its mandate to transform nations through godly influence.

> *Until the Church returns to a Christocentric understanding of leadership, informed by Scripture and modeled through discipleship, it will struggle to fulfill its mandate to transform nations through godly influence.*

In his seminal work 'The Spirit of Leadership', Dr. Myles Munroe asserts that true leadership is concerned more with service and the empowerment of others rather than control. This perspective stands in stark contrast to prevailing worldly paradigms, which often equate leadership with control, coercion, and self-preservation. Christian leadership, by contrast, calls for a radical shift, a commitment to intentional selflessness and effective stewardship. Yet, many who occupy influential positions, whether in government, religious organizations, educational institutions, corporate boardrooms, or institutional hierarchies, remain entrenched in manipulative and control-driven leadership models. The consequence is a culture marked by anxiety, mistrust, and disillusionment. No wonder the phrase 'toxic workplace' has become more than a complaint, it has become a cultural norm. This is the urgent call for leaders to return to the heart of leadership as God intended: not as lords over people, but as stewards of purpose and builders of people.

Furthermore, we must come to the realization that leadership is not just about leading others, it is also about leading our self. Dr. John Maxwell believes that to lead others, we must first learn to lead ourselves exceptionally well. Practically, what does that look like? This includes managing one's emotions, being accountable to truth, and remaining steadfast in one's faith walk. Essentially, a Christian leader is someone who embodies integrity and exemplifies righteousness, not just in public ministry, but in private character. In 1 Timothy 3, the Apostle Paul outlines clear criteria for church leaders, emphasizing qualities such as being above reproach, self-controlled, and able to lead his house. This demonstrates that leadership is not about perfection, but about spiritual maturity and a consistent walk with God and it starts at 'home'.

Christian leadership is therefore best defined as influence through Christlike character and service. A leader guides and provides instruction and counsel to those entrusted in their leadership. Leadership necessitates pointing people toward Christ, rather than to us. According to Ken Blanchard and Phil Hodges in the book 'Lead Like Jesus', "because leadership is an influence process... anytime you seek to influence the thinking, behavior, or development of someone...you are taking on the role of a leader."[4]

> *Christian leadership is therefore best defined as influence through Christlike character and service.*

Hence, we must remain forever vigilant in how we are impacting people and understand that if we are acting in the capacity of leader, there is a level of expectation to be upheld. They believe the most effective leadership starts on the inside with a heart posture of a servant desirous of glorifying God while helping others to become who God created them to be. In summary, Christian leadership may be understood as the ability to inspire others to follow the example of Jesus Christ, to prioritize the spiritual well-being of others, and to remain steadfast in fulfilling God's mission on earth, by making authentic disciples all over the world.

The Heart of a Leader

What does having the heart of a leader entail? Simply put, an exemplary leader must possess a compassionate heart, they must care for the sheep they are entrusted with, and they must possess godly character. Christian leadership does not begin with systems or strategy, rather it begins with the heart. This transcends titles, talents, or even theological knowledge. What qualifies a person to lead in the kingdom of God is primarily the posture of their heart.

The heart is the seat of both emotion and intention, and if it is not aligned with God, no amount of leadership skill can compensate.

In Scripture, we are consistently reminded that God is not impressed by outward appearance or any accolades we might receive from people and institutions. In 1 Samuel 16:7, the Lord tells Samuel that man looks at the outward appearance, while God examines the heart. This principle is fundamental to understanding what it means to be a Christ-centered leader. What is the temperature of your heart?

The heart of a leader denotes their internal compass, their character, motivations, spiritual depth, and moral convictions. It is the wellspring from which their actions flow. Proverbs 4:23 admonishes us to diligently guard our hearts because this is where everything concerning our lives comes from. The heart is the seat of both emotion and intention, and if it is not aligned with God, no amount of leadership skill can compensate. This is one of the major disparities between secular and Christ-centered leadership. The former is concerned with strategies that are deemed effective to evoke a response and even action, while the latter digs deeper to examine the nature and essence of such methods.

TRUE LEADERS CONTRIBUTE VALUE

Imagine yourself in a high-stakes executive meeting. The room is charged with energy as colleagues exchange insights and propose bold ideas. You listen intently, pen in hand, absorbing the information and reflecting deeply, not out of hesitation, but out of intention. You are not simply waiting for your turn to speak; you are processing, discerning where your input can make a meaningful impact. Suddenly, the CEO looks in your direction and says, "You must have an opinion." In that moment, the pressure to speak could override the purpose of your presence. But true leaders understand this: meaningful contribution is not about speaking first or most, rather, it is about speaking with clarity, value, and conviction. Leadership is not the noise of many words; it is the weight of wise ones. When you understand this, you learn that silence can be strength, and thoughtful input often carries greater influence than impulsive commentary. Bre in mind though that it also depends on the room. If you are contending with self-absorbed leaders, then they may dismiss your input as conceit. For poor leaders, everything should center around them, including your input. Be vigilant so you do not miss these nuances.

> *"The Christian leader of the future is called to be completely irrelevant and to stand in this world with nothing to offer but his or her own vulnerable self."*
>
> Henry Nouwen

Know also that as a leader, you do not speak merely because the moment demands a sound. You speak when you have something worth saying. Impactful leadership is not measured by how quickly you respond, but by the weight and wisdom of what you bring to the table. The most effective leaders contribute meaningfully because they know the value of their word. They offer insight that shapes conversations, not empty commentary that simply fills space. As a godly leader, do not underestimate the power of your voice. Your word is powerful, make it count for something that adds value to others.

Many leaders fail not because they lack knowledge or opportunity, but because their hearts were not prepared for the weight of leadership. Leadership is responsibility. Conceit, diffidence, bitterness, and the thirst for recognition can quietly corrupt a leader's effectiveness. Jesus warned His disciples about this when He said in Luke 22:26 that the greatest should be like the youngest and the one in charge like the one who serves. This can be uncomfortable for many who assume the role of leadership as it challenges the ego and invites humility into leadership identity. If we are honest with our assessment, those who are enamored with positional leadership struggle with this concept of servanthood as it challenges their zone of power as they perceive it.

Henri Nouwen, in his book, 'In the Name of Jesus,' speaks profoundly to this theme of leading from the heart. He asserts that Christian leadership must transition from relevance to prayerfulness, from popularity to intimacy with God, and from individualism to community. He writes, "The Christian leader of the future is called to be completely irrelevant and to stand in this world with nothing to offer but his or her own vulnerable self."[5] This is a powerful reminder that the heart of a Christian leader must be rooted in spiritual authenticity rather than performance. How do we reconcile this with the way some leaders in the church operate today?

WHEN HONOR BECOMES CONTROL

I once attended a church where the congregation held a deep reverence for the pastor. At first, I saw it as biblical honor, as outlined in Romans 13:1-2, where believers are urged to respect those in authority. Their devotion seemed sincere, especially in how they celebrated him, whether for his birthday, his return from a trip, or even for small achievements. There was always some gesture of admiration, and in many ways, that felt beautiful. Still, I remained somewhat guarded. I never officially became a member. Something within me hesitated, though I could not quite articulate why.

After over a year of consistent attendance, I felt led to host a conference, one intended to edify the Body of Christ.

Though the event was held outside of the church and was not directly affiliated with it, I informed the pastor and assumed I had his support. As the date approached, I began to notice a troubling silence. Unlike other events hosted by members, mine received no mention, no promotion, and no visible support. It puzzled me, given the culture of celebration I had observed so often.

When I finally inquired, I was stunned by the response. The pastor told me that because I had not been "faithful," he could not allow the members to support the event. According to his assessment, I had not demonstrated enough commitment to warrant backing from the church. In that moment, something became unmistakably clear. His reaction revealed a posture of control, not grace. Rather than encouraging Kingdom collaboration, he allowed personal offense or unmet expectations to cloud spiritual discernment.

To develop the heart of a leader, one must engage in consistent spiritual disciplines such as prayer, worship, reflection, and obedience.

The decision exposed an insecure form of leadership disguised as authority, one that measured worth by loyalty instead of calling. He even told me that I did not understand authority. Despite what my flesh was telling me, I managed to responded gracefully indicating that I was still learning. And you know what, I continue to learn because it is a lifelong habit that we all must hone. To date, I still love the church and will continue to support it but I have to remove myself from that unhealthy environment. Here is the lesson to take from this: Know when your environment no longer serves God's purpose for your life.

Authentic servant leadership, the kind Jesus modeled, is not rooted in ego or territorialism. It lifts others, celebrates their callings, and prioritizes the unity of the Body above personal preference. Christian leaders must engage in consistent introspection to ensure their motives align with the heart of God. When support is withheld as a form of punishment or control, it signals a deviation from Kingdom leadership into something far more self-serving.

Jesus modeled a leadership heart that was tender yet strong, humble yet authoritative, full of grace yet steeped in truth. He wept with those who mourned (John 11:35), had compassion on the multitudes (Matthew 9:36), and boldly confronted sin and injustice (Matthew 23). His leadership flowed from His love for the Father and His mission to serve others. As Paul reminds us in Romans 12:2, we are to be "transformed by the renewing of [our] mind," which begins with a yielded heart. Without inner transformation, outer influence will be shallow at best and destructive at worst.

In 'The End of Me,' Kyle Idleman challenges believers to embrace the paradox of leadership in God's Kingdom, where brokenness leads to blessing, and surrender produces strength. He noted, "Jesus became real when... I came to the end of me."[6] He points to the beatitudes in Matthew 5 as a blueprint for godly influence, emphasizing that **the heart submitted to God is the heart qualified to lead.** In substance, the heart of a Christian leader is characterized by humility before God, compassion for other people, purity of motives, a hunger for righteousness, and a willingness to serve without recognition. When leaders attend to the condition of their heart, they reflect Christ, not just in their actions, but in their very essence. The effectiveness of Christian leadership, therefore, depends not only on what a leader does, but who they are becoming in the presence of God.

The Leader's Moral Compass

When considering a moral compass, you should reflect on the internal guidance system that shapes human behavior, decision-making, and integrity. The term itself is both metaphorical and deeply instructive. The word 'moral' pertains to the discernment between what is right and what is wrong, an ethical framework that informs personal conduct. A 'compass,' by contrast, is an instrument used for navigation, designed to point consistently toward 'true north' regardless of external conditions. Together, the phrase 'moral compass' suggests an internalized standard of righteousness that, like a physical compass, provides direction in the face of complexity, confusion, or even cultural drift. For the Christian leader, this compass must be calibrated not by public opinion or personal ambition, but by the unchanging truth of God's word.

Every great leader must therefore have a direct internal standard, a value system that directs their choices, shapes their character, and defines how they respond under pressure. For the Christian leader, this value system is not derived from cultural norms or personal preferences. It is grounded in the invariable truth of God's word, revealed through the written word, and refined through the Holy Spirit. In Proverbs 11:3, the Bible declares, "The integrity of the upright shall guide them: but the perverseness of transgressors shall destroy them." This verse captures the profound truth that it is integrity, not ambition, charisma, or gifting, which sustains a leader. One may observe that at the heart of a leader's moral compass, often understood as their value system, lies the quality of their character. As Ryan Franklin puts it, "character is more than just morals, because character is what defines the internal morals of a person."[7] It is character that shapes ethical discernment, governs responses under pressure, and reflects the depth of one's internal convictions. In times of crisis, controversy, or temptation, a well-calibrated moral compass becomes the anchor that holds a leader steady.

Conversely, secular leadership models often reward results and relationships over righteousness. In fact, the latter seldom ever factor into the equation. In the Kingdom of God, how we lead is just as important as where we lead people. This may help to illuminate why many Christians encounter significant tension in workplace environments that reward conformity to unspoken rules, often framed as 'playing the game.' In practice, such a framework frequently requires the compromise of personal convictions and the suspension of ethical integrity. My own experience includes character assassination, exclusion, and both overt and covert retaliation for rebuffing such dynamics.

Still, for the Christian leader committed to walking in alignment with God's divine purpose, this tension necessitates a deliberate decision about, what moral code will govern one's conduct when cultural norms conflict with Kingdom values? There is no denying that Christian leadership demands more than results, it demands righteousness. The moral compass of a godly leader is shaped by key values such as honesty, justice, accountability, compassion, and holiness. These values do not shift with public opinion or popularity, they are built on the character of Christ Himself. This is the same character leaders of today must seek to emulate.

> *There is no denying that Christian leadership demands more than results, it demands righteousness.*

John MacArthur, in Called to Lead emphasizes that "a leader never compromises the absolutes...a true leader understands that and knows where to hold the line."[8] Moral authority comes from living in alignment with biblical convictions no matter what. It cannot be faked, borrowed, or manufactured, it must be cultivated over time through spiritual discipline and a surrendered life. **A thoughtful example of this kind of moral authority is found in the life of Daniel**. In Daniel 1, we see where Daniel was taken into Babylonian captivity as a young man. There he was immediately immersed in a culture that conflicted with his faith. Yet from the outset, he resolved not to compromise. The word of God says, "Daniel purposed in his heart that he would not defile himself with the portion of the king's meat, nor with the wine which he drank."

(Daniel 1:8) He took a stance internally that manifested externally in spite of the consequences that most certainly would follow, he did not compromise.

> *There will always be opportunities to compromise, especially when no one is watching.*

This was not a matter of personal preference; it was a spiritual conviction. Daniel's refusal to eat the king's food was entrenched in his desire to remain ceremonially pure according to the Law of Moses. Despite the risk to his position, and possibly his life, he held the line where it mattered most. Daniel's steadfast moral posture earned him favor with God and respect from others, including even the pagan rulers. His consistent spiritual discipline, evident in his refusal to stop praying even when it was outlawed as seen in Daniel 6:10, demonstrated that his authority came not from title, but from honesty and spiritual integrity.

Daniel's life illustrates that moral authority is the byproduct of private faithfulness that becomes visible in public leadership. It was this internal alignment with God's truth that empowered him to influence kings, interpret visions, and lead with distinction across multiple regimes. As Christians in leadership, this is how we should seek to represent Christ in the earth. Do it even if it is hard. Let your values speak!

There will always be opportunities to compromise, especially when no one is watching. Whether it is mishandling finances, abusing power, taking credit that belongs to others, or quietly excusing sins in oneself or others, the pressures of leadership often expose what lies beneath the surface. That is the reason the word of God repeatedly calls leaders to live blameless. (1 Timothy 3:2). Not perfect, but above reproach, intentional about living out the gospel they preach.

The story of Joseph in Genesis offers a powerful example of a leader who upheld his moral compass even when no one else was watching. When tempted by Potiphar's wife, Joseph came to the realization that he could not compromise and risk sinning against God. (Genesis 39:9). His integrity cost him a position, but it preserved his destiny. Christian leaders must understand that God rewards integrity in private long before He promotes in public. What are you doing in your sphere of leadership that may well be harming your destiny?

Maintaining a strong moral compass also means being accountable, not just to God, but to others. Leaders must choose to welcome correction, surround themselves with wise counsel, and resist the temptation of inaccessibility. This may call for a daily commitment to self-assessment and a readiness to adjust as soon as any departures are identified. As Dr. Myles Munroe writes, "cultivating the spirit of leadership is a choice and only you can make it."[9] This means, **no one can force you to be a leader of integrity.** A Christian leader's moral compass points to Christ as 'true North.' Everything; decisions, relationships, and leadership practices, must align with His teachings. When a leader operates from this place of inner conviction and spiritual alignment, their leadership becomes not just effective, but eternal in its impact.

Identity in Christ

Until you know who you are in Christ, you will continue to search for affirmation in places that cannot sustain your worth. Hence, understanding who you are through the lens of God's truth is the foundation of Christ-centered leadership. It secures you in purpose, guards you from performance-driven living, and empowers you to lead from a place of wholeness rather than need. Without this foundation, leaders are vulnerable to guiding from a place of insecurity, comparison, or a craving for approval, all of which distort the heart of

Kingdom leadership. When a leader does not know who they are in Christ, they may try to prove their worth through performance, rely on external validation, or even drift into roles and responsibilities they were never called to carry. Effective leaders must possess a clear understanding of their identity, specifically, how God sees them and in whom they live, move, and have their being (Acts 17:28).

While it is uncommon for someone to be asked directly, what is your identity? Most individuals have, at some point, responded to questions such as "What is your nationality?" or "Where are you from?" with a reference to their country of origin. These responses, though valid, are often rooted in cultural or geographical identifiers. However, if one reflects beyond the surface, without necessarily delving into philosophical abstraction, it becomes evident how transformative it would be if, when asked such questions, Christians could respond confidently and authentically from a place grounded in their identity in Christ. Such an understanding is not only foundational for personal formation, but essential for effective and enduring leadership.

'Identity in Christ' refers to a believer's understanding of their worth, purpose, and place in light of what God says about them in Scripture, rather than what the world, others, or personal insecurities indicate. It entails acknowledging that you are a new creation in Him (2 Corinthians 5:17), and that your past no longer determines your destiny. It confirms that you are profoundly loved and fully accepted (Romans 8:38-39), and that you were made to carry out God's predetermined good works as established in the book of Ephesians. This identity enables you to lead from a place of divine affirmation rather than one of striving or diffidence by grounding your sense of value in the immutable reality of God's Word. When leaders fully understand this, they stop trying to prove themselves and instead lead with clarity, assurance, and confidence because they are based on who God has already declared them to be.

DO YOU DEFINE YOURSELF FROM A TRAUMA LENS?

Studies indicate that approximately 61–80% of individuals have experienced some form of traumatic event in their lives. In many cases, these experiences profoundly shape their thought pattern, particularly in how they perceive themselves, their worth, and their capacity to thrive. Trauma, when unhealed, often becomes a filter through which people interpret identity, purpose, and even leadership potential. Now, imagine if you will, a person who looks at themself through the lens of past trauma; betrayal, rejection, or failure. Each wound becomes a mirror, distorting how they see their worth, their capacity, and their calling. Instead of viewing life through God's promises, they filter it through pain, assuming they are unworthy, unseen, or disqualified. They may carry titles or responsibilities, yet still wrestle with internal voices that say, "You are not enough," "You will never measure up," or "They will leave just like before**." When this becomes the framework for identity, leadership turns into performance, affirmation becomes a drug, and fear drives decisions**.

Identity shaped by trauma imprisons, but identity shaped by healing liberates.

Now, contrast that with someone who sees themselves through the lens of Christ. That person leads not to gain approval but because they are already approved. They are no longer held hostage by past experiences or human opinion. Their worth is no longer negotiable. Instead, they lead from a place of healing, precision, and purpose. They understand that their value is not earned but inherited as a child of God. This juxtaposition reveals a powerful truth: **identity shaped by trauma imprisons, but identity shaped by Christ liberates.**

Christian identity begins with understanding that we are not defined by our roles, titles, achievements, or where in the world we come from, but by our relationship with God. In 1 Peter 2:9, believers are reminded that we, "are a chosen generation, a royal priesthood, an holy nation, a peculiar people; that ye should shew forth the praises of him who hath called you out of darkness into his marvellous light:" This identity is not achieved, it is received from God through grace. It is only when leaders embrace their divine character that they can lead with confidence, grace, and spiritual authority.

> *Leaders grounded in Christ know that their value is not in how many people follow them, but in how faithfully they follow Jesus.*

I realize that many leadership failures can be traced back to a crisis of uncertainty about their identity. When leaders do not know whose they are, they often misuse their influence. They may seek control rather than service, or lead from ego rather than calling. This is why Jesus' leadership model is so powerful, He never questioned who He was. Before performing a single miracle or preaching His first sermon, He heard the Father say, "This is my beloved Son, in whom I am well pleased" (Matthew 3:17). That affirmation became the anchor for His ministry. Likewise, Christian leaders must lead from the security of sonship, not the pressure of performance or worldly approval. This identity gives them the freedom to serve rather than strive, to lead with boldness without arrogance, and to face criticism without crumbling under it or having to deem it unsustainable.

Leaders grounded in Christ know that their value is not in how many people follow them, but in how faithfully they follow Jesus. This has been a personal area of struggle for much of my early life. I vividly recall the internal trepidation and apprehension I would experience whenever I was subjected to scrutiny or even when I sensed the possibility of impending criticism. As I got older, I came to appreciate that criticisms are inevitable, and I had to learn to put them into perspective instead of allowing them to overshadow the ongoing work Christ has been performing in me. Besides, some criticisms are untenable and as you grow, you should learn to distinguish that.

While this is not to suggest that all forms of criticism are inherently invalid or should be dismissed, it is essential to exercise discernment. One must pause to consider not only the nature of the critique, but also the channel through which it is delivered, and more importantly, how it resonates with the heart of someone whose identity is firmly rooted in Christ. In 'Maximizing Your Potential,' Dr. Myles Munroe emphasizes that discovering purpose is impossible without understanding identity. He writes that God is the manufacturer of human beings who were created to dominate the earth and, "you cannot effectively release your potential if you do not discover God's purpose for giving your life."[10] Identity in Christ, knowing whose you are, is the launching pad for walking in purpose and purpose is where true leadership begins.

Kyle Idleman, in 'The End of Me,' also points to the paradox of Christian identity; that only when we die to self can we truly live. A leader's power comes not from self-confidence, but from Christ-confidence, which serves as the unshakeable assurance that they are chosen, equipped, and called by God Himself. Understanding one's identity in Christ produces stability in seasons of change and resilience in adversity. We will explore this further in Chapter 5.

> *When the storms of leadership come, and they will,*
> *those who are grounded in Christ will not be shaken.*

When the storms of leadership come, and they will, those who are grounded in Christ will not be shaken. They lead from a place of spiritual security, not emotional instability. The leader who knows who they are in Christ reflects Him in how they lead. They are not afraid to be honest with those in their close circles, and more than that, they are also not afraid of reactions to such honesty. They do not lead to prove themselves, they lead to serve the purposes of God in their generation (Acts 13:36). This is the essence of authentic Christian identity.

Leading on Purpose

Leadership that lacks purpose is easily swayed, shallow in impact, and unsustainable. In contrast, true Christian leadership is inherently purposeful, it is driven by a divine calling designed to bring glory to God. We are not talking about those who assume leadership roles in the church without appreciating that sustainability is contingent on calling. Leading on purpose means more than having goals or a vision statement about where you see yourself in the next two, five or ten years. It means aligning your leadership with God's will, living intentionally, and stewarding your influence in a way that reflects the heart of Christ.

Believers are not the product of random creation, but of God's deliberate design created according to His likeness and with dominion over everything.

Purpose is not discovered by leaders but unearthed through relationship with God. I once completed a seven-day challenge designed by my friend who is a Christian Life Coach.

The challenge was intended for those who desire a deeper and closer relationship with God. Even though it was only for seven days, just my consistent action of setting aside time to meet with God daily, started to make me feel closer to him and my days began to seem more purposeful. In 'The Purpose Driven Life,' Rick Warren opens with the now-famous line: *"It's not about you."*[11] As discussed earlier, that single truth reorients leadership from self-centered ambition to God-centered mission. A Christian leader does not lead to fulfill personal dreams alone, but to realize Kingdom assignments which transcend self.

> *Dr. Myles Munroe powerfully stated, the greatest tragedy in life is not death as some may believe, but life without purpose.*

Ephesians 2:10 states, "For we are his workmanship, created in Christ Jesus unto good works, which God hath before ordained that we should walk in them." This means our purpose is not random or reactive, it is preordained. Here, Paul emphasizes the divine origin and purpose of the believer's identity. The term 'workmanship' comes from the Greek: 'poiēma' which means, "what is made, workmanship, creation: things that are made."[12] This suggests a work of art or a well-crafted creation and speaks to intentionality, as though each of us is a divine poem, crafted with purpose.

Believers are not the product of random creation, but of God's deliberate design created according to His likeness. The phrase 'created in Christ Jesus' speaks to the believer's new identity, formed through union with Christ by grace. This new creation is not passive but instead it is designed 'unto good works,' meaning that purpose is embedded within identity. These good works are not invented by the believer; rather, they are 'before ordained,' pre-prepared by God as the path believers are to actively walk in. This verse affirms that identity in Christ is not only redemptive but also missional: we are saved for something and that is, to fulfill God's purpose on the earth through living lives of faithful obedience and service.

This truth leads us to a deeper understanding: **God is the source, and we are the resources He designed to fulfill His purpose in the earth.** Dr. Myles Munroe powerfully stated, the greatest tragedy in life is not death as some may believe, but life without purpose. Your purpose cannot reside within the confines of your abilities, resources, or experiences alone. If it did, it would not require faith. Purpose requires growth. It requires you to reach beyond your current understanding and surrender to the One who authored your assignment before you ever took your first breath. Because your purpose originates with an eternal God, it carries eternal weight. It is designed to outlive you, to bear fruit long after your earthly journey ends. This is Kingdom design, not ambition.

Still, many drift through life, unaware of the divine intention behind their existence. That my friend is a tragedy. How many people do you know who are just listlessly wandering through life without a sense of purpose? Every gift, every experience, every opportunity has been woven into the fabric of God's greater plan. So, why do so many fail to realize this? When a leader grasps this truth, their actions become more intentional, their influence more impactful, and their leadership more enduring. Part of my own Kingdom assignment is to help others walk their way back to what God preordained for them. To lead on purpose is to be clear about your 'why.' It is to wake up each day with the conviction that your influence matters because it is attached to a divine assignment.

> *Leaders who lack clarity of purpose often become discouraged, distracted, or overly dependent on results for validation.*

Leaders who lack clarity of purpose often become discouraged, distracted, or overly dependent on results for validation. But those who understand their God-given purpose lead with consistency, resilience, and impact, even when results are not immediate. In 'The Principles and Power of Vision,' Dr. Myles Munroe explains that **vision is purpose in action.** He writes, "vision is foresight with insight based on hindsight."[13] Purpose gives birth to vision, and vision provides the blueprint for leadership decisions. Without it, leaders are vulnerable to burnout, judgement, and compromise.

Jesus led with firm purpose. In John 6:38, He pointed out that He did not come down from heaven to do His own will but the will of God. This radical obedience to God's purpose defined Jesus' leadership. He knew His assignment, He pursued it with clarity, and He finished it with conviction. In the same way, Christian leaders today are called to discern their unique 'work' and pursue it deliberately and faithfully. Leading on purpose also requires courage, the bravery to say no to distractions, to resist the pressure to conform, and to stay committed even when the path is unpopular or difficult.

The apostle Paul modeled this in Acts 20:24 by showing complete surrender to God's mission. He was not shaken by opposition or concerned with preserving his own life. His only focus was to finish the assignment God gave him and to do it with joy as we will see in Chapter 7. In this verse, Paul expressed firm devotion to his divine mission. Unmoved by external threats, he valued obedience over self-preservation. His aim was to fulfill his God-given assignment with delight, reflecting a leader whose life was steeped in determination, not comfort.

Paul's leadership legacy was shaped by purpose instead of popularity. Furthermore, we see from his experience that purpose-driven leadership is contagious. When a leader walks in clear calling, they inspire others to do the same. They create environments where vision is cast, values are upheld, and people are mobilized to pursue their own God-given destinies. This is how discipleship and multiplication happen, not by accident, but by leaders who live and lead on purpose. In summary, leading on purpose means:

A. Knowing your divine assignment

B. Aligning your daily actions with eternal goals

C. Refusing to be derailed by distractions

D. Concluding your race with faith and focus

When leaders lead on purpose, they lead with power; not the world's power, but the transformational power of God working in and through them. That kind of leadership creates lasting impact, influencing lives in ways that continue to bear fruit long after the leader has stepped away.

CHAPTER 2

LEADERSHIP DEVELOPMENT

Becoming the Leader God Has Called You to Be

"You cannot lead anyone else farther than you have gone yourself."

— John C. Maxwell

This statement speaks to the foundational truth that Christian leadership begins within. Take a moment to think about this and you will realize that taking care of the inner parts is paramount to effective 'self' and 'other' leadership. Before a leader is called to impact others, they are first called to be conformed to the image of Christ. Maxwell's quote challenges you, the leader to examine the depth of your spiritual maturity, your capacity for self-leadership, and your consistency in walking out the very truths you wish to impart. Simply put, you must do the inner work by taking the path first before you ask anyone else to.

The indisputable need for spiritual discipline lies at the heart of this chapter. Without first developing a strong and genuine connection with God, a Christian leader cannot bear the burden of vision, accountability, or the confidence of others. It took me some time to realize this fact; it was the result of introspection and personal struggle. After I accepted that, my whole outlook on leadership changed. I realized that having a healthy inner life, rather than having talent or drive, is what gives you the strength to lead effectively.

Your soul is strengthened for the rigors of spiritual leadership through prayer, Bible study, deliberate fasting, and submitting to divine accountability. This path is not always simple; in fact, it can be challenging and lonely at times. But a leader is developed in those obscure moments and areas. You must first rise beyond the fleshly wants in order to lead effectively in the spirit. In my experience, the secret place is where true leadership starts. This is buttressed by scripture as we see in Psalm 91:1.

This is echoes powerfully in 1 Timothy 4:7-8, where Paul instructs Timothy, "Exercise thyself rather unto godliness. For bodily exercise profiteth little: but godliness is profitable unto all things, having promise of the life that now is, and of that which is to come." The word "exercise" comes from the Greek gumnazō, meaning to train or discipline, and it implies rigorous effort and consistency. Paul is not dismissing physical training but rather placing emphasis on the surpassing value of spiritual formation. He reveals a principle: that godliness is not inherited, it is developed. And it holds weight beyond the present age into eternity.

As we explore what it means to become the leader God has called you to be, it is important to understand that this journey is not only about influence, but also about intimacy with the Father. It is about being shaped in private before you are sent out in public. Leaders are not simply called to do great things; they are called to become godly people and that 'becoming' starts here.

Spiritual Disciplines of a Leader

It was a bitterly cold morning in the dead of winter in New York City. I was wrapped in a thick blanket, desperately trying to shield myself from the chill. But no matter how hard I tried; I could not shake the draft seeping in through the only door that separated me from the brutal cold outside. I had just stepped away from my desk after hitting a wall with my writing and decided to take a nap, but sleep would not come, I was simply too cold. I remember suddenly feeling overwhelmed by a wave of self-pity and frustration. How did I end up in this predicament? And worse, how was I going to get out of it?

> *To develop the heart of a leader, one must engage in consistent spiritual disciplines such as prayer, worship, reflection, and obedience.*

Then, seemingly out of nowhere, a question dropped into my spirit: "Are you leading yourself well?" I was startled. What? Where did that come from; and what did it have to do with me shivering and trying to fall asleep? Yet, even in that moment, I knew it was God. He was calling me higher, reminding me to take responsibility for what He had entrusted to me. Even in my discomfort, I sensed a divine nudge to rise, to lead myself better. When we learn to discern the voice of God, we can hear him anywhere and in any situation. In this case he was calling me to 'do' better.

Christian leadership is as much about becoming as it is about doing. It is a call to personal transformation, not merely professional activity as some would like us to believe. Effective leadership in the Kingdom of God is the byproduct of a deeply formed spiritual life. Just as Jesus withdrew regularly to pray (Luke 5:16), the Christian leader must cultivate personal disciplines that strengthen their relationship with God and deepen their spiritual capacity to lead others. So, what are **spiritual disciplines**? They are intentional practices that align a leader's heart, mind, and soul with God's will. They are deeply concerned with spiritual conversion which ultimately begins in the mind. Without these disciplines, leadership becomes dry, performative, and vulnerable to pride, manipulation, or burnout. But with the right practices, a leader is constantly being renewed, guided, and empowered by the Holy Spirit. Some of the most foundational spiritual disciplines include the ones outlined below. Of course, this is not an exhaustive list but the ones listed have become increasingly more transformative in my Christian journey. They are also sanctioned by many Christian writers who see the value in honing certain key disciplines in their leadership life.

PRAYER

Prayer is essentially the lifeline of a Christian leader. It is where we clarify our vision, surrender our burdens to the Lord and receive His divine guidance and wisdom. Jesus, though fully divine, modeled a lifestyle of prayer, often withdrawing to solitary places to commune with the Father (Mark 1:35, Luke 6:12). This regular practice of prayer empowered Him to lead with compassion, discernment, and authority. This begs the question, **if Jesus who was fully God and without sin saw value in prayer and intentionally engaged in it, what are we waiting for?** Why are some of us so inconsistent in our prayer lives when He modeled such a clear result-yielding example for us? We must understand that prayer is not optional, it is a non-negotiable.

> *"To abandon prayer is to fight the battle with our own resources."*
>
> Donald S. Whitney

In the book 'Spiritual Disciplines for Everyday Life,' in discussing the role of prayer in spiritual warfare, Donald S. Whitney contends that, "to abandon prayer is to fight the battle with our own resources."[14] It really means going into battle unprotected or insufficiently protected. Prayer brings clarity to our decision-making, peace in times of pressure, and strength when facing opposition from the enemy. Prayer also aligns the leader's agenda with God's will, ensuring that our leadership remains spiritually grounded, and we are always protected. This is why He urges us to pray without ceasing. (1 Thessalonians 5:17). I have come to the conclusion that prayer is the single most important key that unlocks heaven's door.

There are many Christians who maintain that prayer is the outlet through which heaven and earth holds conversations. I am not talking about one off conversations with a stranger like a telephone operator when you encounter a problem with say your electronic device. Rather, it is the regular meaningful conversations such as the ones you would have with your friend or partner. Prayer then speaks to relationship with God that includes consistent speaking and listening on our part. One of the things I would often talk to my social media followers about is the amount of noise around us. It often drowns out the one voce we should be attuned to, that is, the voice of God. **In a world brimming with noise, prayer is God's invitation to stillness, to presence to be still and know with utmost assurance that He is God**.

Though I mentioned speaking with God during prayer, know that God does not need our words, He desires our hearts. This is why He says, "But when you pray, go into a room, close the door and pray to your Father, who is unseen. Then your Father, who sees what is done in secret, will reward you." Matthew 6:6 (NIV) Notice the operative word here is 'when'. This indicates that prayer is not an optional activity but an expected discipline that God has called us to engage with. Chapter 4 sufficiently drives home this point in the section entitled, 'The Power of Prayer'. Through this practice, burdens are exchanged for peace, fear for faith, and isolation for God's presence. At first, it may seem like nothing is happening, it may even appear as an exercise in futility but do not give in to anxiety at this point because God is hearing you. Here is his reassurance for you, "Do not be anxious about anything, but in every situation, by prayer and petition, with thanksgiving, present your requests to God." Philippians 4:6 (NIV). God is cautioning us not to allow anxiety to cause is to forgo prayer as this will result in extricating us from Him. On the other hand, when we leverage prayer as a tool to hear from God and to communicate our needs to Him, He will hear us and supply according to His riches in glory. (Philippians 4:19).

STUDYING AND MEDITATING ON THE WORD

Chapter 1 already tells us that God's word provides moral direction and divine wisdom. This is further bolstered by scripture. Joshua 1:8 instructs, "This book of the law shall not depart from your mouth, but you shall meditate on it day and night... For then you will make your way prosperous, and then you will have good success." (ESV). Here we see a central principle for spiritual success and effective leadership. The command that the Word should not depart from our mouths emphasizes the importance of continual engagement with it, not only through reading but through verbal confession and teaching. The call to "meditate on it day and night" suggests deep, sustained reflection, indicating that God's word must shape both thought and behavior. The conditional promise at the end of the verse reveals that true success, as defined by God, is directly linked to obedience. This verse underscores that prosperity in leadership is not self-generated but flows from a life immersed in submission. That is, learning to step back and allowing God to be your guide. It also requires that you trust Him wholeheartedly.

> *true meditation is not simply reading to gain understanding, it is preaching the Word to your own soul and intentionally applying it to your life, one decision at a time.*

I do not suggest that meditating on God's Word daily comes easily. I have started and stopped more Bible reading plans than I can count. Yet, I have never let go of the deep, persistent desire to commune with God through His Word. Over time, I have learned that true meditation is not simply reading to gain understanding, it is preaching the Word to your own soul and intentionally applying it to your life, one decision at a time. That is where transformation truly begins. Scripture is more than inspiration; it is meant to guide us in our daily walk. Like a map through unfamiliar territory, when followed diligently, it leads you, almost without fail, to the destination God designed for your life. As Psalm 119:105 declares, "Thy word is a lamp unto my feet, and a light unto my path" (KJV). **The Word does not always reveal the full journey, but it illuminates the next step.** And that is often all we need to walk confidently by faith.

FASTING

Fasting is a spiritual discipline that humbles the flesh and heightens spiritual sensitivity. It is a form of consecration where the leader intentionally sets aside physical comfort to draw closer to God. In Matthew 6, Jesus does not say, "if you fast," but "when you fast," indicating that fasting is a normal part of spiritual life that we should not forego. This discipline increases our dependency on God and allows for greater revelation and breakthroughs. Many leaders in scripture, including Moses, Elijah, Esther, and Jesus Himself, fasted during times of transition or major decisions. In the book of Esther where interestingly, the word 'God' does not appear once, we see where Esther leveraged the power of fasting to give her the boldness and courage to go before king Ahasuerus. Not only that, but her obedience resulted in a decision that favored her people.

This tells us that fasting is not only a necessary spiritual discipline, it yields timely and often tangible results.

> *Without spiritual discipline, gifting will outrun character and eventually, collapse.*

For the Christian leader, fasting is a powerful reset and reminder that leadership must flow from divine strength, not human striving. There are several other spiritual disciplines such as worship and rest which operate to make a Christian leader more effective. All these serve as the training ground for Christian leaders. Just as athletes must train their bodies, leaders must train their spirits. These practices do not make someone a leader, but they sustain the leader they have been called to become. **Without spiritual discipline, gifting will outrun character and eventually, collapse.** Leaders who intentionally cultivate spiritual discipline, do not just lead from skill, they lead from a place of divine power and clarity. That is the kind of leadership that leaves a lasting impact.

The way I see it, prayer, meditation on the Word, and fasting were never meant to function in isolation. They form a sacred triad, each amplifying the other. Prayer opens the heart to God's voice. Meditation on His Word grounds that voice in truth. Fasting silences the noise so both can rise above the distractions of life. Without this alignment, fasting becomes little more than a hunger strike. But when all three work together, they create a powerful atmosphere for divine instruction to take root, inner renewal, and spiritual breakthrough. This is not meant to me just another religious routine; it is Kingdom discipline. And it is through this rhythm that Christian leaders are formed, refined, and empowered for eternal impact.

Key Laws of Leadership

Leadership does not operate in a vacuum; it possesses guiding principles that make it effective. While Christian leadership is rooted in spiritual foundation, it is also governed by principles that determine effectiveness. Just as the natural world operates according to the laws of gravity, motion, and sowing and reaping, etcetera, so too does leadership. These vital laws of leadership help guide Christian leaders in how they serve, influence, and build the Kingdom. Relying heavily on John Maxwell's foundational work, particularly, his books, 'The 21 Irrefutable Laws of Leadership' and 'The 5 levels of Leadership', this segment highlights several core leadership laws that align with biblical values. Though not exclusive to Christian literature, these principles are very much applicable in the context of Christ-centered leadership.

THE LAW OF THE LID

This is the first law that Maxwell discusses in 'The 21 Irrefutable Laws of Leadership" where he contends that how well a person succeeds turns on their ability to lead. This is where the concept of the lid comes in. A person reaches their acme in effectiveness if they are unable to lead. In the same way, it is not possible for a Christian leader to grow a church or ministry beyond their personal leadership capacity. Maxwell says, "you can find smart, talented, successful people who are able to go only so far because of the limitations of their leadership."[15] This limitation may stem from believing that you know enough and do not need to persist in learning to ensure your leadership abilities continue to expand.

Proverbs 1:5 tells us that a wise person is inclined to hear and increase their learning and someone who possesses understanding will intentionally pursue knowledge. The scripture is emphasizing that those who are truly wise remain lifelong learners, seeking guidance and Instruction to deepen their understanding and strengthen their leadership. To raise the lid on their leadership, Christian leaders must remain ardent students of the word, of growth principles, and of themselves.

THE LAW OF INFLUENCE

Maxwell contends that, "if you don't have influence, you will never be able to lead others."[16] In short, leadership requires the aptitude to garner cooperation from others through healthy persuasion or control over outcomes and rewards. However, when it comes to true leadership, influence goes far beyond this. It involves the ability to inspire and motivate others to shift their beliefs, behaviors, and attitudes in order to achieve a particular goal or outcome. This reveals that influence can be wielded either positively or negatively. Ultimately, the direction it takes depends on who sits at the helm and how they choose to steward their sphere of influence.

> *Leaders today must understand that their influence begins with credibility, trust, and authenticity.*

If you look at the life of Jesus Christ, He was easily the most influential leader of all time. Why do I say this? Well, unlike most leaders of today who would not be taken seriously outside of their plethora of accolades and accomplishments, Jesus did not need earthly titles to change lives. His presence, compassion, and truth drew people to follow Him. Leaders today must understand that their influence begins with credibility, trust, and authenticity, not control. In Matthew 5:16, Jesus said, "Let your light so shine before men, that they may see your good works, and glorify your Father which is in heaven." This is one of my favorite scriptures as it is not about us at all. It helps us realize that influence in the Kingdom of God on earth is not concerned with spotlighting the leader, but pointing others to the Father through the light emanating from the uncompromised leader who understand their role and influential capacity.

THE LAW OF PROCESS

"A leadership position can be received in a day, but leadership development is a lifelong process."[17] In order for a Christian leader to remain effective, they must think beyond the position and understand that they must grow their leadership every day. Just as physical muscles grow through consistent training, leadership capacity expands through daily, intentional development. Christian leaders must embrace the process of growth, especially when it is slow, painful, or inconvenient.

Paul reminds us in Philippians 1:6 that God is faithful and will surely complete the work He started in us.

Spiritual maturity and leadership capacity are formed over time through wins, losses, corrections, and seasons. There are simply no shortcuts to sustainable, Christ-centered leadership. There is only the daily decision to grow, to submit, and to be shaped by the hand of God. **True influence is never built overnight.** It is the fruit of daily obedience, refined character, and firm faith. Christian leaders must trust the process, embrace the stretching, and remain faithful, knowing that God is working through every step to prepare them for greater influence.

THE LAW OF NAVIGATION

Maxwell proffers that just about anyone is able to steer a ship but only a leader can plan and execute the course. This is what distinguishes a visionary leader from a positional one. A visionary leader plans, prepares, and leads with foresight. They are the ones that anticipate challenges and assist others in navigating change with calmness and clarity. In the book of Nehemiah, we see a clear example of this principle in effect. Nehemiah did not just inspire people to rebuild; he assessed the situation, strategized, and mobilized teams to work toward the vision. The interesting thing about him is that as John MacArthur puts it, "Nehemiah was nobody very special as far as the people of Jerusalem were concerned."[18] Yet, he was so spiritually equipped that he learned to take initiative and engage in strategic decision making when it was most needed.

> *The laws of leadership provide practical guardrails that help Christian leaders stay effective, intentional, and aligned with Godly principles.*

Likewise, Christian leaders must seek God's wisdom first, before making strategic decisions and operate from a place of trusting God with all their hearts. (Proverbs 3:5). The laws of leadership provide practical guardrails that help Christian leaders stay effective, intentional, and aligned with godly principles. While spiritual disciplines shape the inner life, these laws shape the outer application of that leadership. Together, they form a powerful foundation for those called to lead by faith and apply godly wisdom. This list of laws is not exhaustive, but the four laws mentioned here are fundamental to effective Christian leadership.

Accountability and Integrity

Leadership has many essential safeguards that are necessary for anyone called to lead in the Kingdom of God. Such include accountability and integrity without which leadership becomes dangerous. Accountability and character then are not just buzzwords, they are instrumental for leadership to become sustainable and align with God's heart. The Bible makes it clear that God values character over charisma. In Titus 1:7-8, Paul describes a leader as one who must be irreproachable and slow to anger. This person must have self-control, be sober, pleasant, and sanctified. Notably, these are not job descriptions, they are character requirements that serve as God's standard for leaders.

> *The Bible makes it clear that God values character over charisma.*

One of the greatest dangers to leadership is seclusion. When a leader becomes unreachable or uncorrectable, they are vulnerable to moral failure, poor decisions, and spiritual deception. Accountability provides the necessary checks and balances that help keep them steeped in truth and consistent growth. It allows leaders to operate within a structure that serves to strengthen them. Proverbs 27:17 reminds us that, "iron sharpeneth iron; so a man sharpeneth the countenance of his friend." Accountability invites others into your life to ask tough questions, challenge blind spots, and provide much needed spiritual and emotional support. Being accountable to yourself and others is not meant to be vain rhetoric that people with leadership titles throw around to make themselves feel effective. It has meaning and when actively engaged results in a positive impact on the people leading and those being led.

> *Being accountable to yourself and others is not meant to be vain rhetoric that people with leadership titles throw around to make themselves feel effective.*

In "Mentoring Leaders," Carson Pue underscores the vital role of peer-level relationships in the life of a leader. He argues that every leader needs someone who is unimpressed by their title or accomplishments, yet deeply committed to helping them grow in alignment with God's will. Genuine accountability is not merely about having someone to report to, it is about choosing to live with honesty and transparency within a trusted community. Strong accountability structures may include a spiritual mentor or overseer, a leadership team or board of elders, peer relationships with fellow leaders, and access to confidential counseling or coaching. These systems help guard the heart, sustain integrity, and provide wise counsel when the weight of leadership feels overwhelming. Even Jesus, though without sin and completely divine, modeled interdependence. He lived in close relationship with His disciples, invited them into His most intimate moments, prayed alongside them, and continually submitted to the will of the Father. His example teaches us that isolation is not a mark of strength, but a potential threat to it. If Jesus led in community, so must we.

> *Fundamentally, integrity is the embodiment of who you are when no one is watching.*

Integrity on the other hand is about consistency between belief and behavior, living what you preach. It means what you do in private matches what you say or profess in public. Fundamentally, integrity is the embodiment of who you are when no one is watching. Psalm 15:2-4 paints a vivid picture of the person who dwells in the presence of God who is the epitome of integrity. "He that walketh uprightly, and worketh righteousness, and speaketh the truth in his heart. He that sweareth to his own hurt, and changeth not." This scripture outlines the moral character of the one who may dwell in God's presence, emphasizing integrity in both action and inner thought. The passage also highlights the value of solid commitment, keeping one's word even when it is personally costly, a mark of true righteousness and covenantal faithfulness. This kind of leader keeps their word, lives righteously, and refuses to be swayed by bribes or popularity. They lead not for applause, but for obedience.

In the book "Spiritual Leadership," J. Oswald Sanders notes, "...the spiritual leader must be sincere in promise, faithful in discharge of duty, upright in finances, loyal in service, and honest in speech."[19] In short, the Chistian leader must be integrous. They carry a sacred responsibility of charting a course for others to follow. Their words carry weight, and their actions model the gospel, whether they intend to or not. Accountability and integrity are not optional, they are central and cannot be compromised or negotiated away. Without them, leadership becomes a performance. With them, leadership becomes a testimony. **Christian leaders are called to live above reproach, not to impress people, but to reflect Christ.** As stewards of influence, they must walk in truth, stay connected to others, and be willing to submit their lives to God and community. It is not always easy, but it is always worth it.

Leading with Humility

Leadership without humility becomes self-serving. Humility is the heart posture that keeps a leader grounded, teachable, and aligned with God's purpose. Understand that this is not a weakness, it is spiritual strength under regulation, a strength that resists pride, embraces servanthood, and places the mission of Christ above personal ambition. In Philippians 2:3-

5, Paul gives us a clear mandate for leadership when he urges us not to allow anything to be done through strife or for vanity. Paul entreats us to put others first much like Christ did. In order to do that, we must have a Christ-like perspective. The scripture calls believers to reject selfish ambition and pride, urging them instead to adopt a stance of humility that prioritizes others above self. Verse 5 anchors this attitude of meekness in the example of Christ, whose selfless servant-hearted mindset is the model for all Christian leadership.

> *To reject humility is to reject wisdom. It is to lead from pride rather than purpose, and in doing so, risk misleading those we are called to serve.*

In today's culture, humility is often mistaken for weakness or a lack of confidence. However, nothing could be further from the truth. Jesus Christ, the greatest leader to ever walk the earth, modeled humility not as a passive trait but as a powerful force for transformation. His life teaches us that humility is not just a virtue, it is a non-negotiable for effective leadership. To reject humility is to reject wisdom. It is to lead from pride rather than purpose, and in doing so, risk misleading those we are called to serve. As we will see in this chapter, scripture is clear in establishing that pride positions us against God, while humility aligns us with His favor and direction. If your view of leadership excludes humility, now is the time to release that mindset. Discard it, not only because it is unbiblical, but because it will ultimately hinder your ability to lead yourself and others effectively.

Jesus chose the path of humility. He washed feet, welcomed the outcast, corrected with compassion, and ultimately sacrificed Himself for the sake of others. This is the standard of leadership in the Kingdom. According to author C. Gene Wilkes in his book, 'Jesus on Leadership' "the most important quality of Christian leadership...is not a leadership of power and control, but leadership of powerlessness and humility in which the suffering servant of God, Jesus Christ, is made manifest."[20] Christian leadership is not focused on gaining authority, status, or control. Instead, it centers on leading with humility, vulnerability, and a servant's heart. The leaders who truly reflect Christ are not those who seek to dominate, but those who follow His example by sacrificing, serving others, and depending on God's strength rather than their own. Through this kind of leadership, the character of Jesus, the suffering servant, is made visible.

John Maxwel conceptualized leadership in the context of influence. Now, I would like to venture to say that humility is the foundation of godly influence. A scripture I quote often to myself and others as a reminder to walk in humility is James 4:6 which states that, "God resisteth the proud, but giveth grace unto the humble." A proud leader may rise quickly, but they will fall just as fast even when it does not seem like it. A humble leader, however, gains access to divine grace, insight, and spiritual authority that cannot be manufactured by any theory or framework.

> *Those who wish to excel in leadership must understand the need to be faithful to the trust of those who look to them for guidance.*

Leaders who operate with humility have certain traits that poise them for impact in leadership. Dr. Myles Munroe states that, "true leaders readily embrace submission to authority and are conscious of their stewardship of the trust given to them by those whom they serve."[21] He is simply saying that those who wish to excel in leadership must understand the need to be faithful to the trust of those who look to them for guidance. They should not focus on what pleases the leader themselves to the exclusion of those poised to follow them. Humble leaders listen quickly but are slow to speak, are willing to make mistakes, open to correction, and are comfortable lifting others. The upshot of this all is that true humility does not operate to diminish a leader's confidence, rather, it anchors it in God rather than their dangerous ego.

> *Rather than asserting authority over others, true greatness is expressed through servanthood, a voluntary lowering of oneself, or for the sake of others.*

In many secular settings, humility is often mistaken for indecisiveness or weak-mindedness. But Christian leadership reveals the paradox, the lower a leader bows, the more impactful their influence becomes. Jesus said, "Whoever wants to become great among you must be your servant" Matthew 20:26 (NIV). I have always found this scripture profound and instructive to my spiritual growth. Here, Jesus redefines the concept of greatness within the Kingdom of God, contrasting it with worldly notions of status and dominance. Rather than asserting authority over others, true greatness is expressed through servanthood, a voluntary lowering of oneself, or for the sake of others. This verse challenges leaders to embrace humility as the path to influence, making service, not power, the hallmark of Kingdom leadership.

Humility is the secret strength of effective Christian leadership. It is not about denying one's gifts but about surrendering them to God for the benefit of others. Humble leaders are not insecure; they are secure in their identity in Christ, which frees them from the need to dominate or defend their position. Their value is not in status, but in service. When leaders lead with humility, they create trust, safety, and transformation in their communities. More importantly, they reflect the very nature of Christ, the ultimate Servant-Leader.

In summary, this chapter affirms that Christian leadership is not driven by strategy alone but by intentional alignment with the word of God. Effectiveness flows from a disciplined spiritual life, one grounded in prayer, Scripture, fasting, and practices that shape the leader's heart and character. As we explored foundational leadership principles such as the Laws of the Lid, Influence, Process, and Navigation, it became clear that these timeless truths mirror biblical wisdom and offer a framework for faithful leadership. The chapter also emphasized the essential roles of integrity and accountability, reinforcing that character—not charisma— sustains lasting impact. Ultimately, humility emerges as the hallmark of Christlike leadership, where influence is anchored not in power, but in service. Together, these insights underscore that Kingdom leaders are not only called to lead effectively but to be spiritually formed and accountable in all they do.

CHAPTER 3

LEADING WITH GODLY WISDOM

Understanding the Emotional Dimensions of Leadership

"Leaders must either invest a reasonable amount of time attending to fears and feelings, or squander an unreasonable amount of time trying to manage ineffective and unproductive behavior."

– Brené Brown

Browns's sentiment expressed here captures a reality many Christian leaders underestimate. Emotions do not disappear just because they are ignored. In fact, when unattended, they often resurface in unhealthy ways disguised as burnout, conflict, or decision fatigue. Brown's insight challenges leaders to realize that tending to emotional well-being is not weakness. It is wisdom. It is also deeply biblical. Jesus Himself never dismissed emotions, He acknowledged grief, embraced compassion, and even wept openly. One powerful example of this in action occurred in a mid-sized church in North Carolina that my friend Julie was introduced to when she first moved there in the fall of 2017. She was quickly identified as a dedicated follower of Christ and was soon asked to become the church secretary. This went well for a while until the lead pastor, after serving faithfully for more than twenty years, began noticing a growing sense of detachment among his team. Interestingly, Julie had noticed the same thing upon joining the ministry but did not say anything seeing she was the newcomer.

As time progressed, miscommunications escalated, and staff turnover increased. It was not until he participated in an emotional intelligence workshop that he realized he had been suppressing his own emotional fatigue for years, and it was silently shaping how he led. That revelation sparked an internal shift. He shared the training with his team and began to engage with them differently, asking questions, creating space for vulnerability, and processing his own challenges with a counselor. The culture of the church gradually transformed as their trust was rebuilt. The staff became more unified, and the leader himself became more present and spiritually refreshed.

Julie's story is a modern-day parable of Proverbs 4:23, which tells us, "Keep thy heart with all diligence; for out of it are the issues of life." The Hebrew word translated 'keep' here is natsar, which means, "to guard or watch over closely." It implies calculated effort. Why? Because everything a leader does, every interaction, every decision, every response, flows from the condition of their heart. Emotional health, then, is not optional for the Christian leader, it is foundational and must never be ignored.

In this chapter, we will explore the emotional layers of leadership, emotional intelligence, discernment, the role of spiritual maturity in decision-making, and the effect these have not only on the leader but on the community, they are called to serve. When emotional wisdom partners with spiritual depth, the result is leadership that is both empathetic and effective, solidified in God's truth and tuned to the real needs of people.

Biblical Foundations of Wisdom

In a world filled with the clamor and clatter of busyness, rapid change, and conflicting opinions, wisdom is the defining trait that sets Christian leaders apart. More than knowledge or education, biblical wisdom is the ability to discern God's will and act accordingly. It is spiritual insight embedded in truth, fueled by humility, and empowered by the Holy Spirit. When we read the book of Proverbs, we see a plethora of references to wisdom. In fact, this book is often referred to as the 'Book of Wisdom.' Proverbs 4:7 says, "Wisdom is the principal thing; therefore get wisdom: and with all thy getting get understanding." This powerful verse elevates wisdom as the foundation for all effective leadership because it determines not just what a leader knows, but what a leader does with what they know. The Hebrew word for "wisdom" is ḥokmā which means, "wisdom, skill, learning...spiritual things."[22] This conceptualization transcends intellectual knowledge; it refers to skillful, practical, God-centered living. It is the ability to apply knowledge in a way that honors God and blesses others.

Even to the most faithful among leaders, wisdom and understanding are not automatic.

Hence, when Solomon who is presumed to be the writer of Proverbs, refers to wisdom as, "the principal thing," he is saying wisdom is preeminent and therefore must be prioritized above all other aspects of a leader's attributes. To "get" wisdom then implies intentionally seeking to acquire it, thus signifying effort and possibly even cost. "Understanding" in this scripture speaks to discernment, insight, and the ability to distinguish between things. It is a deep perception that comes from reflection and spiritual clarity. Even to the most faithful among leaders, wisdom and understanding are not automatic. If it was, why would God entreat us to "get" them? Therefore, they must be actively and sacrificially pursued, often at personal cost.

The verse also implies that these are spiritual gifts worth more than gold or silver as expressed in Proverbs 3:13-15. Proverbs 4:7 teaches us that wisdom should be a believer's highest pursuit because it leads to life, favor, and spiritual maturity. In areas of leadership such as parenting, ministry, and personal decisions, this verse challenges us to elevate divine wisdom above worldly gain, and to continually pursue understanding in all things.

> *While knowledge can be obtained through study, wisdom is often the result of experience, spiritual maturity, and deep relationship with God.*

As we examine the biblical foundations of wisdom, it is important to distinguish it from mere knowledge as we know it. Knowledge accumulates facts and puts them together to declare what we purport to know. Wisdom on the other hand applies to the truth. While knowledge can be obtained through study, wisdom is often the result of experience, spiritual maturity, and deep relationship with God. James 1:5 exhorts believers who lack wisdom to ask God, with the assurance that He will give generously without reproach. It is fitting that a God who exalts wisdom as preeminent (Proverbs 4:7) would eagerly respond to a sincere and faith-filled request for it.

> *Wisdom is not a tool for manipulation, but a sacred responsibility to lead others according to God's heart, not human opinion.*

I vividly remember the moment this truth became personal for me during my second year as an undergraduate law student. At the time, asking God daily for wisdom, knowledge, and understanding had become a fixed part of my morning devotion. One morning, mid-prayer, it was as though the Holy Spirit gently interrupted my routine with a probing question: "Why are you asking for what you already possess?" In that moment, I experienced what can only be described as an epiphany. I realized that God had already granted the wisdom I had long been praying for. My petition shifted instantly, from asking for wisdom to asking God to teach me how to steward and apply it. Though it may sound philosophical, I felt as though a veil had been lifted from my eyes, allowing me to see the world, and my calling through an entirely different lens. This shows that wisdom is not just intellectual, it is relational. It comes from intimacy with the One who knows all things. Christian leaders must continually seek wisdom from the Word, through prayer, and through the guidance of the Holy Spirit.

> *Christian leaders must continually seek wisdom from the Word, through prayer, and through the guidance of the Holy Spirit.*

It is also important to note that the Bible is the primary source of wisdom for the Christian leader. God's Word provides guidance, clarity, and direction in life. Biblical wisdom teaches leaders how to handle conflict with grace (Matthew 18:15-17), how to lead with integrity (Proverbs 11:3), how to plan with discernment (Proverbs 16:9), and how to remain rooted in truth amidst cultural confusion (2 Timothy 3:16-17). The Bible also offers countless examples of wise leadership, from Moses' delegation in Exodus 18, to Solomon's judgment in 1 Kings 3, to Jesus' profound discernment in dealing with both followers and opponents.

In the "The Baker Illustrated Bible Background Commentary," Duvall and Hays emphasize that biblical wisdom literature, especially Proverbs, Ecclesiastes, and Job, offers leaders a framework for making godly decisions in complex situations. They noted for instance that, "self-restraint in speech is a common value in the instructional wisdom texts."[23] These texts speak to the moral, emotional, and spiritual dimensions of leadership in ways that are timeless. In addition to being a discipline, wisdom is also a spiritual gift. 1 Corinthians 12:8 identifies the "word of wisdom" as one of the manifestations of the Spirit. This gift is crucial for leaders who must discern motives, navigate tension, or make high-stakes decisions. It is especially important in counseling, conflict resolution, and organizational direction. However, the gift of wisdom must be stewarded with humility. Wisdom is not a tool for manipulation, but a sacred responsibility to lead others according to God's heart, not human opinion.

Biblical wisdom is the cornerstone of Christian leadership. It governs how leaders think, act, respond, and guide others. It transcends trends, political correctness, and surface-level success. Leaders grounded in the wisdom of

God will be steady in uncertainty, discerning in chaos, and compassionate in conflict. Without wisdom, leaders react. With wisdom, leaders respond with clarity, courage, and grace and therein lies all the difference.

Emotional Intelligence

In the modern leadership landscape, especially in ministry and church contexts, emotional acumen is no longer optional, it is essential. Emotional intelligence or emotional quotient (EQ) refers to a leader's ability to understand, manage, and respond to emotions, both on their own and others', with wisdom and empathy. For the Christian leader, EQ is not just a soft skill, it is a spiritual discipline, one that reflects the relational nature of Christ and enhances a leader's influence, credibility, and care for people. According to Ryan Franklin, "the way we communicate with and relate to others is often a product of a different type of mental clarity called' emotional intelligence."[24] Our emotions are actually signals that inform us of what is transpiring internally. Hence, it is to our benefit to be aware of how our emotional responses impact those around us. In the context of industries, companies, and religious organizations such as churches, it is imperative to prioritize EQ as it intensifies interpersonal effectiveness and serves to improve our leadership productivity and success.

> *Our emotions are actually signals that inform us of what is transpiring internally.*

Franklin also references the work of psychologist Daniel Goleman who wrote the books 'Emotional Intelligence' (1995) and 'Working with Emotional Intelligence' (1998). He outlines key benefits of emotional intelligence (EQ) that are especially relevant for leaders. Goleman identifies five core components: self-awareness, self-regulation, motivation, empathy, and social skills.

These are not merely psychological principles; they align closely with biblical values and are deeply applicable to Christian leadership. For example, self-awareness reflects the biblical call to examine oneself (2 Corinthians 13:5), while self-regulation mirrors the fruit of the Spirit, particularly self-control (Galatians 5:22-23). Motivation rooted in purpose rather than ego, empathy that reflects Christ's compassion, and social skills that foster unity and peace all point to a leadership model built on Scripture and spiritual maturity. An individual who is keen on effectively leading need not only understand these key components but ascertain how they may employ them daily.

SELF-AWARENESS

This factor is the cornerstone of EQ and is concerned with knowing yourself. In other words, it is the ability to recognize and understand your own moods, emotions, and drives, as well as their impact on others. Before a leader can lead others well, they must first comprehend what is happening within themselves. This includes recognizing their emotional triggers, strengths, weaknesses, and motivations and then assessing how to navigate them. The key characteristics that would enable them to do this are emotional insight, accurate self-assessments, and self-confidence.

> *As Goleman sees it, self-aware individuals are not just in touch with their feelings, they understand them and know how those emotions affect their behavior and performance.*

As Goleman sees it, self-aware individuals are not just in touch with their feelings, they understand them and know how those emotions affect their behavior and performance. They do not allow their emotions to hijack their actions, but instead use them as data to guide decisions.

David's honest reflection in Psalm 139:23-24 is a model of self-awareness when he said, "Search me, O God, and know my heart: try me, and know my thoughts: And see if there be any wicked way in me...." Here, David invites God to examine his inner life, his heart, thoughts, and motives, for any hidden sin. It models a leader's willingness to be vulnerable before God, pursuing not only correction but guidance toward righteousness and lasting alignment with God's will. Self-awareness allows Christian leaders to totally depend on God who will enable them to lead with humility, authenticity, and self-restraint, avoiding emotional outbursts or reactive decision-making.

SELF-REGULATION

Self-regulation involves managing your emotions with spiritual insight so they do not control you or affect those around you negatively. Self or emotional regulation as some characterize it does not mean suppressing emotions, but rather channeling them constructively. Key elements of self-regulation include self-control, trustworthiness, adaptability, and conscientiousness. Leaders with heightened self-regulation are able to pause, think, and then respond rather than react. This is especially crucial in leadership and crisis, where impulsivity can damage relationships and reputations.

They remain calm under pressure, ae open to change, and are guided by a strong sense of ethics.

> *Leaders with heightened self-regulation are able to pause, think, and then respond rather than react.*

As you know, leadership comes with inevitable pressure, disapproval, and unpredictable challenges. Without emotional control, a leader can respond with anger, fear, or even pride, damaging relationships and undermining trust. Self-regulation allows the Christian leader to pause, pray, and respond, rather than react impulsively. Proverbs 16:32 highlight that a person who is slow to respond with anger and controls his spirit is better than even one who has power and might. This text exalts self-control as a greater strength than physical power or military conquest. It teaches that greatness lies in mastering one's emotions and impulses highlighting that inner discipline is more honorable and impactful than external victories. Spirit-led self-regulation reflects maturity and safeguards both the leader and those under their care.

MOTIVATION

In Goleman's emotional intelligence model, motivation is intrinsic. That is, driven by a deep desire to achieve for the sake of achievement, not for external rewards like money or status. It is predominantly characterized by passion for the work itself, commitment to goals, taking initiative, and optimism even in the presence of failure. For Goleman, emotionally intelligent individuals are intrinsically motivated. They go after their goals enthusiastically and with perseverance. They are not deterred by setback and perceive them as opportunities to enhance their learning rather than hindrances. This is the kind of motivation need to perpetuate resilience and growth.

Here, we must realize that leading from a place of purpose is significantly more powerful than leading from an emotional place. Christian leaders must lead from conviction, not emotional highs, and lows. This means we cannot always take action according to how we feel but based on what is required at a given time. Purpose-driven motivation produces resilience, consistency, and long-term impact, even when things feel difficult or discouraging. Rick Warren reminds us that, "focusing on ourselves will never reveal our life's purpose."[25] The clear inference here is to lend out focus to those we serve Leaders with high EQ are not driven by ego, applause, self-aggrandizement, or emotion. They are secured in purpose, pressing forward because they know who they serve and why it matters. They know that their leadership is about the people they were predestined to serve and not themselves.

EMPATHY

This speaks largely to our understanding of others and their emotional makeup. Empathy transcends sympathy to involve perceiving unspoken feelings and perspectives, and responding with sensitivity. Empathetic leaders are attuned to body language and tone, possess cross-cultural sensitivity, and are service oriented. Goleman believes that empathy is crucial in managing relationships, leading diverse teams, and building trust. He especially emphasized empathy as the most important EQ component in today's global economy because of the increasing need for cross-cultural communication and collaboration.

Empathy then is the ability to feel what others feel, to see situations from their perspective, and respond with compassion. This was a defining trait of Jesus' leadership. In Matthew 9:36, we read: "when he saw the multitudes, he was moved with compassion on them..." Jesus was not indifferent to their pain. He felt it and acted on it. This verse highlights that leadership begins with seeing people, feeling their need, and responding with care. Empathy builds trust, bridges communication gaps, and deepens relational connection. Leaders who demonstrate empathy listen well, lead gently, and build teams where people feel seen and valued. When they have leaders who feel undervalued, the immediately validate their concerns and provide reassurance.

SOCIAL SKILLS

Social skills are all about building healthy relationships and networks. It includes the capacity to find common ground, influence others, and lead teams effectively. Ministry does not happen in isolation, it happens through connection, communication, and collaboration. That is why those with heightened social skills know how to communicate effectively, manage conflict, are great collaborations and effectively leverage their influence.

> *Those with heightened social skills know how to communicate effectively, manage conflict, are great collaborations and effectively leverage their influence.*

Leaders must be able to foster teamwork, and speak truth in love and patience. Ephesians 4:15 calls believers to "speak the truth in love." Great leaders balance honesty with grace, creating cultures where people grow, even through difficult conversations and challenging transitions. Goleman contends that people with strong social skills are often persuasive, good listeners, and skilled at managing disputes. They excel in building rapport and are often described as charismatic, not because of charm alone, but because of their rationale intelligence.

Once, I found myself in a situation where the Human Resources department at a company where I worked attempted to pressure me into taking ownership of a decision to terminate an employee. They framed their request as a means of presenting a united front between HR and senior leadership. When I objected, they shifted the narrative, suggesting their concern was about a leader's inability to have difficult conversations with staff. However, that was not the issue at hand. HR was asking me to compromise my values and integrity by taking responsibility for a decision in which I had no involvement. Even those with exceptional communication skills and strong interpersonal influence must remain cautious not to sacrifice their integrity for the sake of compliance or image. Doing so crosses the line into manipulation and violates the foundation of trust.

Many of the traits found in emotionally intelligent leaders are mirrored in Galatians 5:22-23, love, joy, peace, patience, kindness, goodness, faithfulness, gentleness, and self-control. These fruits are not just signs of spiritual health; they are also key indicators of high EQ. When leaders walk in the Spirit, they lead with emotional maturity. Emotionally intelligent leaders are spiritually grounded, relationally aware, and resilient under pressure. They understand themselves, love others well, and create environments where trust can grow. Christian leaders who cultivate EQ reflect the heart of Christ, who led with compassion, communicated with clarity, and built meaningful relationships with people from every walk of life. Leadership is not just about strategy; it is about soul care. EQ is how leaders care for both their own soul and the souls of others.

Discernment and Decision-Making

I have long come to the realization that leadership lives and dies at the point of decision. Every day, leaders are faced with choices, some small, others life-altering. But not all decisions are black and white. That is the reason Christian leaders must lead with discernment, not just logic. Discernment is characterized by the spiritual ability to perceive direction, and timing through the lens of God's wisdom and the guidance of the Holy Spirit.

While emotional intelligence helps leaders respond well to people, discernment equips leaders to respond well to situations, especially the ones that are not easy to navigate with surface-level wisdom. For example, that time when I have to stand up to HR and let them know I could not be inauthentic at the expense of my integrity as a leader. That took courage but I had no choice that to stand on what I believed in. It was discernment that allowed me to avoid the pitfall of manipulation masquerading as unity.

Discernment, therefore, is both a spiritual gift and a developed discipline.

So, what do you surmise is discernment? Discernment is the ability to distinguish between what is good and what is God. Hebrews 5:14 describes maturity this way, "But strong meat belongeth to them that are of full age, even those who by reason of use have their senses exercised to discern both good and evil." The scripture implies that spiritual maturity is the result of consistent practice and discernment. The "strong meat" symbolizes deeper truths reserved for those who, through continual obedience and spiritual focus, have trained their faculties to distinguish between good and evil, highlighting that maturity is not instant but developed over time through disciplined use. Discernment, therefore, is both a spiritual gift and a developed discipline. It grows over time as leaders learn to listen to God, reflect on His word, and assess motives and consequences with a clear mind and spirit.

Jesus is the ultimate model of discernment. In John 8, when confronted with the woman caught in adultery, He did not react to the crowd's demand for justice. Instead,

He paused, listened, and responded with both truth and mercy when He cautioned the individuals who deemed themselves sinless to throw the first stone at her. (John 8:7). Jesus quickly discerned the heart of the situation, not just the facts. Christian leaders are called to do the same, not just see what is happening, but perceive why it is happening and what impact could result from different responses.

> *Many individuals are expert at wearing masks and if leaders are unable to discern this, they may well align themselves with those poised to thwart their destiny.*

It is also imperative that we examine discernment in leadership practices because this is the venue of most decision making. This starts with discerning **'people'**. John Maxwell contends that, "effective leaders are readers of situations, trends, opportunities, and people."[26] So, who are Christian leaders looking to align themselves with? Not every opportunity is from God, and not every person has pure intentions. Paul warns in 2 Corinthians 11:14 that "Satan himself is transformed into an angel of light." Leaders must be prayerful and Spirit-led when forming teams, selecting mentees, or delegating responsibility. Many individuals are expert at wearing masks and if leaders are unable to discern this, they may well align themselves with those poised to thwart their destiny.

Having discernment as to **'time'** is also vital. Ecclesiastes 3:1 teaches that everything has a season. A crucial decision made at the wrong time can be just as damaging as the wrong decision altogether. Leaders must learn to wait on God's timing and avoid making hasty moves, even when under pressure. As significant as timing is **'strategy'**. Sometimes, what worked in the past may not be what God is blessing now. Just as Joshua had to get new instructions for each battle, Christian leaders must be sensitive to divine strategy rather than leaning on what seems familiar. Finally, discerning God's **'will'**, is perhaps the most significant part of spiritual discernment in decision making. Romans 12:2 reminds believers that a renewing of the mind will help them to prove what is that good, acceptable, and perfect, will of God. Leaders must pursue God's will above personal ambition, popularity, or pressure from others but leaders cannot always see that at the outset if their mindset is out of alignment.

Further, leaders are often expected to make quick decisions, especially in crisis or under pressure. Conversely, Napoleon Hill who is known for his book 'Think and Grown Rich,' contends that successful people make decision quickly and change their minds slowly. I can see how a Christian who having read this book might be swayed especially since Hill came to that conclusion after interviewing over five hundred successful people. Yet, a Christian leader must discern that fast does not always mean wise. The Bible consistently points to pausing, praying, and seeking counsel as part of sound decision-making. Proverbs 11:14, for example, we are told that people will fall in the absence of counsel but will find safety where there is an abundance of counsel. Christian leaders should cultivate a network of trusted advisors and mentors and remain open to correction and feedback. Spiritual maturity is shown in a leader's willingness to listen before leading.

> *Christian leaders should cultivate a network of trusted advisors and mentors and remain open to correction and feedback.*

Through this study, I realize that leaders who leverage the tools they have at their disposal are better at discerning and deciding well. These include the word of God, prayer, wise counsel, and the peace of God. Discernment separates wise leaders from impulsive ones. It keeps leaders from reacting to pressure and empowers them to respond with insight and patience. **While knowledge can be learned**

in a classroom, discernment is cultivated in the secret place with God. Christian leaders must not only make the right decisions but to make God-led decisions, ones that align with His will, His timing, and His character.

Impact on the Community

Christian leadership is never confined to pulpits, platforms, or boardrooms, it is meant to transform communities. "A true leader's work is not a job or career but the very life he lives."[27] Leaders who lead lives shaped by godly wisdom do not just make decisions; they create environments where people thrive, faith grows, and the love of Christ becomes tangible. The real measure of leadership is not only in what is accomplished, but in who is impacted and how deeply. Proverbs 11:10-11 tell us that the righteous flourish, there is rejoicing in the city, and a city is exalted by the blessings of the upright. This verse captures the heart of godly influence. When wise and righteous leaders rise up, communities are lifted. Their leadership brings peace, equity, healing, and justice. Yet, we live in a society where many leaders are given to self-serving ways and in so doing negatively impacts the community. Leaders must understand that what they are doing in the present will become their legacy long after they are gone. This begs the question; what kind of seeds are leaders sowing in their communities?

> *Wise leaders sow peace, protect against gossip and strife, and ensure that their teams, congregations, or organizations reflect harmony and strength.*

Wise Christian leaders always consider what kind of mark they are leaving on their community. Through a deep dive into leadership impact on communities, I have found that Christian leaders operating in wisdom impact their communities in four major ways. They create a culture of honor and unity, they champion justice, they empower others to lead and grow and they strengthen spiritual foundations. How do Chistian leaders foster honor and unity? Wise leaders know that division is one of the enemy's favorite weapons. So, they become bridge-builders, uniting people across differences and cultivating environments where people feel valued, seen, and safe. Psalm 133:1 celebrates the coming together of the brethren as it emphasizes the value of unity. Wise leaders sow peace, protect against gossip and strife, and ensure that their teams, congregations, or organizations reflect harmony and strength.

It is also evident that biblical wisdom leads to righteous action, not passive observation. In Micah 6:8, we are told that the Lord requires us to operate with justice, mercy, and humility. Wise leaders stand up for the vulnerable, address systemic injustices, and serve their communities with compassion and courage. They understand that authentic leadership is not just about preaching the Gospel but also living it out practically. In my line of work, I oversee programs that serve the housing insecure (homeless). I see this as a calling, and I guard the welfare of our clients as I do my own. I advocate on their behalf and often serve as their amplifier when their voices are drowned out. Jesus Himself spent His earthly ministry healing the sick, feeding the hungry, elevating the poor, and restoring the marginalized. His leadership was not just spiritual, it was social and transformational.

Wise leaders help people build lives of purpose and faith through intentionally imparting biblical wisdom.

When you lead from a place of wisdom, you multiply your influence. What do I mean by this? Leaders who are looking to positively impact their community, recognize potential in others and create opportunities for growth, development, and shared responsibility. Ephesians 4:12 tells us that leaders are to "equip the saints for the work of ministry, for building up the body of Christ." That means community impact increases exponentially when leaders disciple others to rise and lead in their own right.

This generational mindset ensures that communities are not dependent on one personality but are sustainable, empowered, and future-focused. Furthermore, when a leader walks in godly wisdom, their community benefits from biblical teaching, healthy boundaries, and spiritual vision. Lives are changed through programs as well as encounters. Wise leaders help people build lives of purpose and faith through intentionally imparting biblical wisdom. As Jesus said in Matthew 7:24, "Whoever hears these words of mine and puts them into practice is like a wise man who built his house on the rock." Strong leaders help others build robust and sustainable lives. Leadership is not measured by how high you climb, but by how many others rise because you were there. How many lives were changed because you came this way.

Wise leadership is also marked by foresight, the ability to perceive and prepare for what lies ahead, both for oneself and the wellbeing of others. In Proverbs 29:18, the Scripture declares, "Where there is no vision, the people perish: but he that keepeth the law, happy is he." The Hebrew word for *vision* (*ḥāzôn*) refers not merely to foresight or dreams, but to divine revelation, a word from God that directs and fortifies a people. When leaders lack revelation, direction falters, and communal purpose deteriorates. People begin to flounder because they lack clarity even where there is no shortage of resources. Conversely, intelligent leaders who receive and steward their vision become stewards of life-giving order. They help others see beyond current struggles and align with what God is building.

In this light, the goal of Kingdom leadership is not just preservation but multiplication, of people, of purpose, and of righteousness. Leaders who serve from this place recognize that the greatest gift they can give their community is not control, but clarity; not dominance, but direction. They cultivate future builders, rather than mere followers. Their legacy is not in a name etched on a building, but in lives shaped to withstand the storms of life. Too often do we encounter leaders who miss this crucial element of their purpose. Though they are commissioned to build others and equip them for discipleship, they all their personal desires to supersede what God has ordained.

This is the reason spiritual wisdom must remain the cornerstone of Christian leadership. It discerns the needs of the people, hears the heart of God, and makes decisions that elevate both present outcomes and future generations. Leaders like this who fully understand their roles in the lives of others, do not merely inform; they impart. They cast vision and construct lives that are heartened to withstand the tests of time. One such leader in modern society is John C. Maxwell who has intentionally equipped leaders all around the world with the tools need to lead themselves and in turn others, exceptionally well. Maxwell's understanding of His divine assignment leaves no room for insecurity. He simply knows that he must develop others as part of his earthly kingdom purpose. You need to understand that the same is true for you also and begin to lead with others in mind at all times.

PART TWO:

THE POSTURE OF KINGDOM LEADERSHIP

"You cannot lead others until you have learned to lead yourself."

—Adapted from Proverbs 16:32

CHAPTER 4

SERVANT LEADERSHIP

Leading Like Jesus

"Leadership is not about being in charge. It is about taking care of those in your charge."

– Simon Sinek

Sinek's words echo the very heartbeat of Christ-centered leadership. Today, many aspire to lead because of the attention they received from others and the status associated with their titles. In the age of social media, visibility and titles are preeminent. However, Jesus upends that model entirely. He teaches that leadership transcends mere positional ideals to consider the posture of the heart for service to others.

In John 13, Jesus gives us one of the most powerful illustrations of this principle. In verses 4-5, the Bible records that Jesus rose from supper, laid aside His garments, took a towel, and began to wash the feet of His disciples. This act, typically reserved for the lowliest servant, is carried out by the Lord of Lords. Verse 13 goes on to say, "Ye call me Master and Lord: and ye say well; for so I am." Jesus confirms His title, but He redefines how authority should operate. By stooping to wash their feet, He gives an eternal lesson, greatness in the Kingdom comes through humility, and influence is stewarded through service.

To lead like Jesus means to reject cultural norms of dominance and adopt a model of purposeful care. This requires spiritual maturity and sensitivity. Consider this real-life example. I once volunteered in a large nonprofit organization that catered to the needs of the less fortunate. The executive director was known for her efficiency, strategy, and visionary leadership. However, after a while, her team began showing signs of burnout and disengagement. When she paused to investigate, she realized her leadership had been high on performance but low on presence. She began meeting regularly with her team, not just for planning but for listening. She asked questions about their personal and spiritual growth and created space for reflection and prayer. Over time, the atmosphere shifted. The staff no longer felt like cogs in a machine but valued members of a mission. She had not changed her goals; she changed her posture. She began leading like Jesus.

In Matthew 20:26, Jesus declared, "Whosoever will be great among you, let him be your minister." That word 'minister' is translated from the Greek word 'diakonos', meaning servant. Not simply someone who holds a position in church, but one who actively serves others without expectation of repayment. Jesus defines greatness through servanthood, showing us that leadership is not found in how high we rise, but in how deeply we care. As we move into this chapter, we will explore the dimensions of servant leadership, uncovering how leading like Jesus requires courage, clarity, and compassion. It is about shepherding, not showcasing. It is about building people, not platforms. This is the call of every Christian leader, to not just lead for Christ, but to lead like Him.

> *Jesus defines greatness through servanthood,*
> *showing us that leadership is not found in how high*
> *we rise, but in how deeply we care.*

Leading like Jesus also demands deliberate internal transformation that reflects in external behavior. It is not enough to adopt servant language or mimic compassionate gestures. What makes Jesus' leadership so distinct is that He embodied servanthood at His core. Every act of healing, correction, intercession, or instruction was rooted in love and fueled by intimacy with the Father. His leadership was relational, redemptive, and always sacrificial.

In the book of Philippians, Paul encourages believers to adopt not just the behaviors but the mindset of Christ. He describes how Jesus, though being in the form of God, did not cling to equality with God but made Himself of no reputation and took on the form of a servant. This passage is not simply theological, it is instructional. It teaches that self-effacement is not an add-on to leadership, it is the essence of it. Leaders are called to lay down their entitlement, to take on the mindset of servanthood, and to lead from a place of submission to God's will. Jesus' example calls us to examine our motives and methods. Are we seeking visibility or transformation? Are we building teams or building trust? Are we using our position to empower others or to protect ourselves?

> *Leaders are called to lay down their entitlement, to take on the mindset of servanthood, and to lead from a place of submission to God's will.*

This chapter will guide us through these questions. It will challenge us to reevaluate how we define success in leadership. It will reinforce the truth that the highest form of influence comes from earning trust rather than commanding attention. And it will remind us that Jesus' way, though narrow, is the most impactful path a leader can walk. To lead like Jesus is to become more than a manager of tasks; it is to become a steward of people's souls. And that is a weighty, beautiful calling.

The Shepherd Leader

C. Gene Wilkes proffers that, "servant leaders humble themselves and wait for God to exalt them."[28] Put another way, authentic servant leaders do not pursue their own elevation. Instead, they stay humble and trust God to raise them up in His timing. Jesus, our ultimate example of servant leadership, refers to Himself in John 10:11 as the "Good Shepherd" who gives His life for the sheep. This declaration is not meant to be perceived as poetic. Instead, it teaches us that Christian leadership is rooted in sacrifice, not status.

> *A shepherd leader is someone who leads with compassion, not control.*

A shepherd leader is a person who leads with compassion, rather than control. They know the people they lead intimately, protect the vulnerable and defenseless, guides with wisdom and precision, models humbleness and consistency, and lay down personal gain for the prosperity of the flock. Jesus is the epitome of servant leadership and has set the benchmark for anyone to follow who seeks to lead God's way. J. Oswald Sanders postulates that, "so quiet and unobtrusive is the great Servant's work that many today doubt His very existence."[29] Imagine our God so powerful and yet seeks to hide himself (Isaiah 45:15) instead of taking the pedestal.

The shepherd leader is not aloof, disconnected, or obsessed with platforms. In today's society, we hear leaders talk about their platforms often. Most are concerned with making a name for themselves and ensuring that they are seen. This operates in direct contrast to the shepherd leader. In fact, in the Bible, shepherds were considered one of the lowest ranks of people and nearly everyone ignored or disregarded them. Yet, their position and commitment remain one of the most profound examples of how we should lead. They walk with the sheep, smell like sheep, and are willing to fight for them when danger arises. This leadership model is relational, not transactional as most leaders today make it.

Now you can appreciate that one of the most powerful pictures of leadership in Scripture is not the warrior, the king, or the prophet, it is the shepherd. Interestingly, unlike many leadership approaches, a shepherd leads not with force, but with care. Yet, they lead not from behind, but from in front. Robert Stewart makes reference to Nelson Mandella in his book 'Servant Leadership,' where Mandela proffered that, "it is better to lead from behind and to put others in front, especially when you celebrate victory when nice things occur. You take the front line when there is danger. Then people will appreciate your leadership.[30] Imagine how your leadership character would transform if you decided to prioritize covering and shielding those you lead?

Take a moment to consider the latter part of this quote and you will see that the shepherd leader is really selfless. They lead from in front even in the face of danger with the ultimate goal of protecting their flock. In a world that often celebrates dominating, top-down leadership, the model of the shepherd stands in quiet contrast, strong, protective, and deeply invested in the well-being of others. Still, we cannot ignore the impact of this quote as it captures the essence of servant leadership and reflects a profound philosophy of humility, responsibility, and shared success. Great leaders do not pursue the spotlight or dominate from the top. Instead, they empower others, allowing team members or followers to advance, shine, and contribute meaningfully. A servant leader gives credit to others during moments of success, acknowledging their efforts rather than seeking personal recognition. When challenges arise, strong leaders do not hide behind their teams. They step forward, take responsibility, and protect those they lead. This selfless approach fosters trust and loyalty among those being led. People follow such leaders not out of obligation, but out of approbation and utmost respect for them.

> *Today's shepherd leaders are patient, and they understand that growth takes time, so they do not rush sheep.*

The reference above teaches us that leadership is more concerned with sacrifice, service, and shared strength rather than control or visibility. One of the most compelling examples of servant leadership in Scripture is found in the life of David, particularly in 2 Samuel 24. After David sinned by taking a census of Israel, an act entrenched in pride and a failure to trust God's provision, a plague was released upon the nation as God's judgment. As the people suffered, David did not shift blame or remove himself from the consequences. Instead, he stepped forward in full humility and responsibility. 2 Samuel 24:17 tells us that when David saw the angel who was striking the people, he spoke to the Lord and admitted that he had sinned and done wicked things. However, the sheep had not done anything to deserve God's wrath, so David asked God to mete out the consequences on him and his household instead.

In this moment, we see where David exemplified great leadership. He did not hide behind his authority, instead, like a true shepherd, he took the front line. He pleaded with God to spare the people and bear the consequences himself. This posture of intercession, humility, and self-sacrifice reveals a heart aligned with God's own, a leader more concerned with the well-being of those he led than with protecting his own status. It is no wonder the Lord referred to David as a man after His own heart, selfless and full of grace. David's response offers a striking contrast to the kind of leadership driven by self-preservation. He models the essence of servant leadership, anticipating the greater fulfillment seen in Christ, who stood in the gap for all humanity.

> *We must understand that to lead like Jesus is to lead like a shepherd. And there is no higher calling in Christian leadership than that.*

In today's ministry context, the shepherd leader is accessible in that they do not hide behind title or task, they are available to the people they serve. They are also protective.

They guard their people from spiritual error, unhealthy relationships, and even burnout. Today's shepherd leaders are patient, and they understand that growth takes time, so they do not rush their sheep. They are also focused on Wholeness. They care about spiritual formation, emotional well-being, and long-term fruit in the lives of those they lead. This is echoed in 'Lead Like Jesus' by Ken Blanchard and Phil Hodges, who argue that Jesus' style of leadership was both strategic and servant hearted. He was not just a shepherd in sentiment, He was also intentional, visionary, and transformational.

One of the biggest threats to the ministry of a shepherd leader today is trying to shepherd in a culture of celebrity leadership. In an age where many equate leadership with visibility and branding, the call to be a shepherd leader resists ego and platform-centered leadership. Shepherding is often thankless. It happens in hidden places such as hospital rooms, counseling sessions, prayer closets, long phone calls, and one-on-one discipleship moments. However, it is in those places where real transformation happens. Shepherd leaders leave a deeper impact than public figures because they actually walk with people through the highs and lows of life. We must understand that to lead like Jesus is to lead like a shepherd. And there is no higher calling in Christian leadership than that.

Establishing Balance

One of the most overlooked but critical aspects of servant leadership is the ability to create balance. Ryan Franklin suggests that "most leaders generally lean toward being workaholics. We're obsessed with busyness. It's almost like a medication for us."[31] He admits that for him, getting approval from others is like a drug that he keeps craving. This is a critical factor which must not be discounted. This drive and desire for validation and affirmation can result in a leader's premature demise. As if that is not enough, numerous Christian leaders, driven by compassion and commitment, find themselves pouring out constantly without being poured into. Over time, this leads to exhaustion, spiritual dryness, poor decision-making, and in some cases, total burnout.

> *Leaders must take responsibility for how they utilize their time, establish boundaries, prioritize family and spiritual health, engage in rest and recreation, and say "no" when necessary.*

Balance as we see here is not just about maintaining equilibrium from a work-life perspective. It is also focused on not doing more than you have the capacity to do, in the name of personal glory. While Jesus calls us to lead sacrificially, He never calls us to lead recklessly. Effective servant leadership is not about neglecting yourself for the sake of others; rather, it is about learning how to manage your life wisely so that you can serve others effectively and sustainably. Even in the secular world, "the goal of servant leaders is to strike a balance between fostering the professional and personal growth of their followers and maintaining the momentum of the current purpose."[32] Embedded in this approach is the idea of effective stewardship. A servant leader must leverage the power of his team, providing he chooses them with discernment. He must also recognize that delegation is not a weakness, it is an intentional exercise in wisdom to ensure the best of him is available to shepherd his flock.

Something we can learn from the greatest servant leader in history, Jesus, is that He modeled healthy balance. He constantly demonstrated the importance of balance between ministry and rest. In Mark 6:31, after intense ministry, Jesus told His disciples, "Come ye yourselves apart into a desert place, and rest a while..." Even though crowds were waiting, and needs were urgent, Jesus prioritized withdrawal and rest. He often chose solitude over overexposure and managed His energy intentionally. This reveals that balance is not optional, it is essential. If Jesus made room for rest and renewal, how much more should we? It is evident then that balance is not about living a soft or self-centered life. It is about managing your time, health, and relationships in a way that honors God. Leaders must take responsibility for how they utilize their time, establish boundaries, prioritize family and spiritual health, engage in rest and recreation, and say "no" when necessary.

Dr. Myles Munroe teaches that "you are responsible to guard and protect your potential."[33] The principle of balance is evident here as he is stressing the need to shield your potential from attack and harm implying a balance between your strength to protect and your exposure to attack. Balance enables a leader to lead with joy and longevity, not just intensity. For that to happen, according to Munroe, you must speak about your potential sparingly and only to those who can see the vision. Without intentionally shielding and protecting your potential, the future of your dreams for your life remains susceptible to the enemy's attacks.

It is not difficult to tell when there is an absence of balance. Usually, a leader will begin with the right motives but if not properly stewarded, will slowly drift into an unhealthy rhythm. There are some common warning signs that may trigger a journey down this path and a leader must be alert to them. For instance, feelings of resentment toward the people they are serving, neglect of personal prayer, Bible study, or even family, guilt when resting or saying no, and loss of clarity or passion for their calling. A leader must realize that these are not signs of weakness. They are invitations from the Holy Spirit to adjust, reprioritize, and return to a grace-paced leadership rhythm.

> *A leader must be available for family, friends, and spiritual mentors who refresh and challenge them to maximize their reach.*

How can servant leaders shift from imbalance to establishing a balanced approach? Just as Jesus did often, leaders must choose a day to rest, reflect, and recharge so they can have the strength and clarity of mind needed to be effective. They should practice setting clear boundaries. It is important for a leader to know their limits and protect their 'yes.' Not every need that is brought to a leader's attention is their divine assignment. Also, a leader must prioritize their relationship with God by spending time daily in His presence, not just preparing for others, but feeding their own soul. Investing in relationships is another pivotal way to create balance.

A leader must be available for family, friends, and spiritual mentors who refresh and challenge them to maximize their reach. Finally, a leader should seek to lead from a place of overflow, not obligation. When one's well is full, serving becomes a joy. When it is empty, ministry becomes a burden. Christian leadership is not a sprint, it is a lifelong calling, and that requires rhythms and proper pacing. In Isaiah 40:31, we are promised that those who wait on the Lord will replenish their strength. Therefore, leaders who wait on God, rest in His presence, and protect balance which in turn allows them to lead with greater impact over time. It is important to also note that establishing a balance is not selfish but necessary. A servant leader who honors God through creating a balanced lifestyle will be more present and more effective in every area of their leadership. It is not about doing less; it is about doing what matters most and doing it well.

Nurturing Others

To nurture is to purposefully care for the growth, development, and well-being of other people. In Christian leadership, nurturing is not passive, it is purposeful. Servant leaders do not just lead people to outcomes, they walk with people through processes. They create space for others to flourish, not just function. Jesus did not just give commands, He gave Himself. He modeled patience, empathy, instruction, and correction in ways that fostered spiritual growth and transformation. He expresses lovingkindness and tender mercies towards us whether or not we are deemed deserving. In 1 Thessalonians 2:7-8, Paul describes his leadership this way, "But we were gentle among you, even as a nurse cherisheth her children... we were willing to have imparted unto you, not the gospel of God only, but also our own souls, because ye were dear unto us."

Here, the imagery of a nurturing mother is evident. But Paul does not only compare his ministry to a loving mother but also to a caring father. The care the mother shows is the same word used for birds protecting their eggs by covering them. There is a level of devotion as well as a loving tenderness. This is what the heart of a nurturing leader should look like, someone who sees people as more than roles to fill, but souls that need to grow under guidance and care.

From a Christian point of view, at its core, nurturing is about developing people, not just into followers, but into leaders, disciples, and world changers.

Franklin postulates that in the material world, "few organizations spend the necessary time developing leaders...but organizations that put a focus on development go further with success and usually do it in less time."[34] It takes vision and foresight for an organization to see the value in developing its leaders and yet once they do, they create a culture of growth and longevity. From a Christian point of view, at its core, nurturing is about developing people, not just into followers, but into leaders, disciples, and world changers. The late Dr. Myles Munroe's group of companies known as Munroe Global has a mission to develop followers into leaders and leaders into agents of change. This is exactly what a nurturer does.

Jesus nurtured His disciples by spending time with them daily, teaching them in parables and through life experiences, correcting them with love, empowering them to act, and trusting them with His mission. The Christian leader today is called to do the same by walking closely with others, pouring into them consistently, and calling out their God-given potential. Carson Pue states, "The heart of Jesus's leadership was putting his Spirit in his disciples by mentoring and teaching, and then setting them free to pursue vision, for God."[35] That is what nurturing does, it awakens purpose and cultivates character in leaders as well as those being nurtured.

You can tell a nurturing leader by their actions. They show up consistently and not just to critique, but to celebrate, support, and walk with others through growth. They create space for people to process struggle and ask questions without fear of judgment. This builds trust and fosters emotional and spiritual safety. I have also found that nurturers speak life and truth. They encourage, but they also challenge, believing in the best of others and expecting them to rise to it. Astute leaders recognize that everyone is different, they learn how to nurture according to the needs of the person they are entrusted with nurturing. One of the best examples in the Bible is that of Jesus and His disciples. He nurtured these twelve men who would later become apostles, missionaries and martyrs who did exploits in His name.

> *Astute leaders recognize that everyone is different, they learn how to nurture according to the needs of the person they are entrusted with nurturing.*

In essence, to nurture is to invest in the growth and flourishing of others. It requires time, presence, patience, and intentional care, but the impact it produces is enduring. Servant leaders who commit to nurturing do more than build effective teams; they cultivate whole, healthy, purpose-driven individuals who carry that same spirit of care into every sphere they influence. In a fast-paced culture that often rewards hustle over humanity, nurturing may seem slow or inefficient. Yet, it is the way of Jesus, deliberate, relational, and transformational. As Paul exhorted in 1 Thessalonians 2:7, "But we were gentle among you, even as a nurse cherisheth her children." Here, Paul illustrates the tender, consistent nature of spiritual leadership. He reminds us that nurturing is not a sign of weakness, it is a mark of Christlike strength. It is the kind of leadership that builds people, not just platforms, and leaves a legacy of lasting change.

The Power of Prayer

Prayer is one of the major spiritual disciplines mentioned in Chapter 2 as it is meant to be a staple in the lives of all believers. Here, we are concerned with the role prayer plays as a force in the life of a servant leader where it is not optional but essential. It is the power source, the compass, the place of divine alignment and renewal. Without prayer, even the most gifted leader eventually runs dry. Prayer allows leaders to draw from God's strength instead of their own, leading not just with strategy but with spiritual authority. Prayer is what distinguishes Christian leadership from worldly models. It is not about merely managing outcomes but about partnering with God to better understand your life's purpose and direction. Jesus' entire ministry was saturated in prayer. He prayed before making decisions (Luke

6:12-13), before performing miracles (John 11:41-42), and even in moments of deep exhaustion and grief (Matthew 26:36-39).

In Matthew 6:9-13, Jesus taught His disciples to pray and ultimately demonstrated through His life that prayer was the fuel of leadership. If the Son of God, in all His power, prioritized prayer how much more must we? If prayer was not important, it is not likely that Jesus would have so intentionally outlined the parameters for us to pray. In the scripture, He provides a structured and spiritually rich model for prayer. The prayer begins with "Our Father which art in heaven, hallowed be thy name," establishing both the intimacy and reverence with which believers are to approach God, recognizing His holiness while embracing Him as Father.

> *Prayer quiets the noise of the world and allows the leader to hear the still small voice of God.*

As the model prayer progresses, verse 10 reflects a posture of surrender and alignment with God's sovereign purposes instead of the pursuit of personal agendas. Verse 11 speaks to ongoing dependence on God for daily physical and spiritual provision. While verse 12 underscores the importance of humility, grace, and relational reconciliation in the life of the believer. Finally, the prayer ends with an acknowledgment of the need for divine guidance and protection from moral failure and spiritual attack. The prayer concludes with a doxology of praise and surrender, "For thine is the kingdom, and the power, and the glory, forever." (Mathew 6:13). This ending center all prayer within the ultimate authority and majesty of God. This prayer is not simply a liturgical recitation but a framework for cultivating hearts that are humble, dependent, forgiving, and aligned with God's will. It shapes the leader's prayer life to reflect worship, submission, and accountability.

A leader who does not pray cannot operate with discernment as there is no communication between them and God.

We may consider some of the results of an active prayer life. Prayer quiets the noise of the world and allows the leader to hear the still small voice of God. As in Habakkuk 2:1-2, vision is often birthed or clarified in the secret place. Servant leadership is emotionally and spiritually demanding. Isaiah 40:31 promises that "they that wait upon the Lord shall renew their strength." Prayer is how that waiting happens, and how supernatural strength is received. Prayer provides discernment and alignment in decision making. James 1:5 assures us that God gives wisdom generously to those who ask. Great leaders do not just pray about people, they pray for them, with them, and on their behalf. In John 17, Jesus prayed an entire chapter over His disciples and future believers. That is the heart of a servant leader, covering others in prayer.

Leadership invites spiritual warfare. When you take on the responsibility of influencing others toward Christ, you become a target. Prayer is both defense and offense. Ephesians 6:18 instructs leaders to pray in the Spirit at all times with all kinds of prayers and requests as part of the full armor of God. Through prayer, leaders protect their flock, confront spiritual attacks, and declare God's will over their teams, ministries, and communities. In this sense, prayer serves as an all-encompassing shield and covering for the praying leader.

Leadership without prayer is direction without GPS, ambitious, but easily misdirected.

A prayerful leader builds a prayerful community. Servant leaders set the spiritual tone, if prayer is central in their life, it becomes central in the culture they are cultivating. In The Maxwell Leadership Bible, John C. Maxwell writes, "prayer insists that we quiet our hearts and wait, slowing us down to receive from God."[36] When we pray, we must always leave room to listen so we can hear from God. A leader who does not pray cannot operate with discernment as there is no communication between them and God. Therefore, leadership without prayer is direction without GPS, ambitious, but easily misdirected. Prayer is the engine of servant leadership. It restores, refocuses, and reignites. It reminds the leader that they are not the source, they are the vessel. Through prayer, a servant leader stays connected to the One who empowers them to lead with love and care for others.

CHAPTER 5

NAVIGATING CHANGE AND CRISIS

In Times of Uncertainty

"Anyone can hold the helm when the sea is calm."
— Publilius Syrus

Syrus captures the truth that leadership is not proven in ease, but in adversity. Calm waters reveal very little about a leader's strength, but when the storm hits, character, conviction, and clarity all come to the surface. In times of uncertainty, a leader's foundation is tested, and their example becomes either a source of peace or panic for those who follow them.

One leader who exemplified this kind of steady resolve in turbulent times was the UK Prime Minister, Sir Winston Churchill. When the world was on the brink of collapse during World War Two, Churchill's leadership offered clarity, strength, and resilience to a nation consumed by fear. His speeches were not just strategic;

they were characterized by sheer in moral courage. He famously said, "To each, there comes in their lifetime a special moment when they are figuratively tapped on the shoulder and offered the chance to do something truly great. What a tragedy if that moment finds them unprepared." He was not merely a man of words but a man whose clarity of mission rallied a people to stand when giving up would have been far easier.

> *The Christian leader does not simply prepare for uncertain seasons; they are often called to lead right in the middle of them.*

Spiritual leadership requires that same kind of resolve. The Christian leader does not simply prepare for uncertain seasons; they are often called to lead right in the middle of them. One of the most comforting and instructive scriptures in this regard is Isaiah 41:10. "Fear thou not; for I am with thee: be not dismayed; for I am thy God: I will strengthen thee; yea, I will help thee; yea, I will uphold thee with the right hand of my righteousness." This verse is rich with divine assurance. First, God addresses the common human condition, fear, and counters it with His presence. "I am with thee" is not a cliché; it is a covenant. God then says "be not dismayed," meaning, do not become shattered or broken down by your circumstances. Why? Because He is not only present but actively involved, strengthening, helping, and upholding. The "right hand of my righteousness" symbolizes both power and justice. In other words, when a leader stands in the middle of chaos and clings to God, they are being held by the very hand that governs the entire universe.

Here we will examine what it means to lead when outcomes are uncertain, when plans fall apart, or when the future feels blurry. We will also explore how spiritual disciplines, strategic thinking, and emotional resilience come together to form the backbone of Kingdom leadership in crisis. As you read, you will be encouraged not just to survive uncertain seasons, but to lead through them with faith, wisdom, and the kind of vision that does not come from trend forecasts but from time spent in the presence of the Almighty.

In a Changing World

You have heard it said often, change is constant and that is simply because it is true. Whether driven by culture, technology, politics, or internal growth, change impacts everyone and oftentimes leaders feel it first. Christian leaders must be equipped not only to respond to change but to lead through it with wisdom, vision, and faith. We are living in a rapidly shifting world where societal norms are evolving, and church dynamics are transforming. Also, generational expectations are shifting rapidly. If a leader tries to resist change completely, they risk becoming irrelevant. If they chase every trend, they become unstable. The call of the Christian leader is to remain anchored in truth while adapting in method, hence becoming flexible without compromising.

> *Christian leaders must remain rooted in prayer and the Word to stay steady, communicate with clarity and consistency, acknowledge what is changing while reinforcing what remains unchanging, namely the truth of God, their values, and the divine mission.*

Ecclesiastes 3:1 reminds us, "to everything there is a season, and a time to every purpose under the heaven:" This verse affirms both the inevitability and the intentionality of change. Change is not always chaos it can be an opportunity ordained by God. Some people may think it is impossible to adapt to the changes as fast as they are happening, but this is mainly due to relying on one's own strength to navigate these changes. As Myles Munroe contends in 'Understanding Your Potential', "the people who change the world are the people who have taken impossible out of their dictionaries."[37] The Apostle Paul came to this realization early in his ministry when he declared in Philippians 4:13 that he could do all things through Christ who afforded him strength. The bottom line is, nothing is impossible with God and even the most difficult changes can be navigated with Him at the center.

Yes, the world is constantly changing but leaders cannot succumb to the pressures of these changes. In seasons of transition, people look to leadership for direction, stability, and reassurance. If leaders are crumbling under pressure, then where will the people go? This is the reason must fortify themselves with prayer and other spiritual disciplines such as fasting and meditating on the word of God.

> *Christian leaders must embrace lifelong adaptability, not out of fear, but out of faithfulness to the evolving needs of those they serve.*

Whether it is organizational restructuring, cultural shifts, or global crises, the leader becomes the emotional and spiritual thermostat of the group. Therefore, Christian leaders must remain rooted in prayer and the Word to stay steady, communicate with clarity and consistency, acknowledge what is changing while reinforcing what remains unchanging, namely the truth of God, their values, and the divine mission.

A leader must also inspire hope and a vision for what is ahead, even when the path seems uncertain.

In 'Leader Shift,' John Maxwell emphasizes the need for leaders to learn, unlearn, and relearn in response to inevitable changing times. He posits that, "you cannot be the same, think the same, and act the same if you hope to be successful in a world that does not remain the same."[38] Christian leaders must embrace lifelong adaptability, not out of fear, but out of faithfulness to the evolving needs of those they serve. A leader must be in a constant state of updating if they want to 'move with the tides' and maintain a rhythm that is in-sync with the changes. Sometimes, this may mean getting rid of old ways of doing things to make way for the new which maintain the integrity of what is being done.

There is a plethora of biblical examples of individuals who had to navigate tough changes. Take Moses for example. He had to lead an entire nation through a drastic, identity-shifting change, from slavery to freedom as seen in the book of Exodus. Exodus 3:11 tells us that Moses had serious doubts about his ability to execute the daunting task until God assured Him that He would be with Him. Leaders must operate with the same assurance that is with them in the toughest of transitions. Another notable example is

Esther who had to discern how to influence power structures in a politically volatile moment. Esther 4:14 shows us a challenge given to Esther by Mordecai who was sufficiently assured that God would send help, yet he dared her to consider whether she was the outlet for that change to come through. Esther rose to the occasion and was successful in obtaining the favor of the king.

It is almost a travesty to explore biblical leaders who had to navigate difficult changes without considering the Apostle Paul. Paul constantly adjusted his methods to reach Jews, Gentiles, intellectuals, and commoners, while never compromising the gospel as seen in 1 Corinthians 9:22 where he declared that he was, "being made all things to all men that he might save some." Talk about a leader who was adaptable. One thing these leaders had in common was they feared change enough to become immobilized. They saw it as a divine opportunity to step into purpose and did not hesitate to follow through.

Change often comes with crisis but the latter can operate as a catalyst for the power of God to become evident. In the Kingdom, crisis does not cancel calling, it often refines it. Romans 8:28 declares that "all things work together for good to them that love God…" Wise leaders recognize that crisis reveals character, refocuses vision, repositions people and releases innovation and spiritual authority. Even in the toughest of circumstances, purpose must prevail with an understanding that things will soon change. Remember, change is constant. In Tough Times Never Last, But Tough People Do, Robert H. Schuller notes, "every problem has a limited lifespan."[39] With God, even the worst disruptions can become divine redirection.

In a changing world, Christian leaders must be adaptable to change. They should not panic when things get hard and the way to do this is to stay in a state pf preparation. In addition, they should not just survive crisis, they help others grow through it. Leadership in a changing world is not about staying comfortable but remaining steadfast in faith while embracing the changes as they come.

Strategic Leadership

In times of uncertainty, it is not enough for leaders to be spiritually grounded, they must also be strategically equipped. In the year 2022, I authored a book called, 'The Strategic Goal Setting Handbook' with a view to helping individuals who wanted to develop personal to a practical tool to realize this. Since then, I have had the opportunity to teach these dynamics in schools, colleges, and universities in the United

States and the Caribbean and here is what I have discovered. Strategy is how vision becomes action. It is how faith takes form. Christian leaders must learn to plan with wisdom, act with clarity, and lead with foresight, especially when navigating change, crisis, or complexity.

Luke 14:28 gives us something to ponder. According to this verse, if someone wishes to build a tower, it makes sense that they would first sit down and assess the cost to ascertain whether they have enough to see it through to completion. If this is not one of the greatest levels in strategic leadership, I do not know what is. Spiritual passion without strategy can lead to confusion and ineffective leadership but with the right approach all this can be averted. Also, know that strategy is not unspiritual, it is wise stewardship.

> *Spiritual passion without strategy can lead to confusion and ineffective leadership but with the right approach all this can be averted.*

What then is Strategic Leadership? This is the ability to see ahead while staying grounded in the present, make decisions that align with long-term goals, anticipate obstacles, and prepare accordingly, mobilize people, systems, and resources toward vision, and adapt plans without losing purpose. In short, it is visionary leadership. In the Principles and Power of Vision, Dr. Myles Munroe shared a story of a little girl who was lifted up by her father while aboard a ship, so she could look over the horizon, once the little girl got a glimpse of the vastness of what was in front of her in the distance, she excitedly exclaimed, "I can see farther than my eyes can look!"[40] This is the summation of strategic leadership, to envision more than that which is visible to the naked eye.

Christian leaders who are strategic take a proactive posture; they do not wait around for crisis to force change. They seek God's direction, study their context, and act with intentionality. I often get asked this question, "Shauna-kaye, why are you doing that...?" Only to later hear from the same source, "oh, now I see why you did that." God has blessed me with the ability of foresight and as a strategic leader, I do not take it for granted. I recognize the need to leverage it as a platform for effective, Christ-centered leadership.

The Bible provides a blueprint for strategic leadership as exemplified through several outstanding leaders who demonstrated strategic thinking. Genesis 41 tells us that Joseph, even in crisis, created a plan to save Egypt from famine by storing grain in advance. This is a leader who had foresight and did not wait for the crisis to transpire before taking action. According to Mark 6:7, Jesus sent the disciples out in pairs delegated authority, and empowered others long before He left the earth. His leadership was not only spiritual, but it was also intentional and scalable. Here is the essence of the blueprint, envision and outcome and then take steps to be able to navigate it successfully when it arrives.

> *Strategic leaders focus on what matters most, even when pressured to do everything. In short, they leverage the power of structure and systems.*

There are some core traits of strategic Christian leadership that when leveraged will be a game changer for leaders. Firstly, the leader must always be ready to assess. A strategic leader constantly asks, "is this plan moving me closer to what God called me to do?" The is necessary because strategy must serve the God-given vision. Secondly, a strategic leader must become adept at clarifying their priorities. Not everything urgent is important. Strategic leaders focus on what matters most, even when pressured to do everything. In short, they leverage the power of structure and systems.

Most people who know me know that I love systems simply because they are effective. The third trait is to leverage systems. Effective strategy involves structures, communication flows, accountability layers, and sustainable rhythms. It is not just who does what, but how things work together. Fourthly, strategy is not about micromanaging, it is about trusting the right people with the right responsibilities. As Moses learned from Jethro in Exodus 18, delegation is wise leadership. Finally, strategic leaders pay attention to trends, feedback, and facts, but they also listen for God's voice in decision-making. Spirit-led strategy honors both reason and revelation.

Some assume that strategic planning competes with trusting God, but that is a false dichotomy. Strategic leadership is how faith is stewarded. Proverbs 16:9 says, "A man's heart deviseth his way: but the Lord directeth his steps." The key is to plan faithfully but stay open to God's redirection. Dr. Myles Munroe emphasizes this in The Spirit of Leadership, saying, dependable leadership is about having the capacity to inspire others through encouragement, motivated by a passion, generated by a vision, and shaped by a conviction, kindled by a purpose. Strategy helps deliver that inspiration with clarity and consistency. In essence, strategic leadership is faith in motion. It is Spirit-led thinking, intentional planning, and courageous execution. It helps leaders navigate uncertainty, mobilize people, and build sustainably.

Maintaining Faith in Difficult Seasons

Leadership is not generally tested in times of comfort and ease. However, in challenging times, leaders are presented with the opportunity to refine their skills. Crisis, change, loss, and prolonged uncertainty can rattle even the strongest leaders. However, Christian leaders are called to stand firm in faith, not because they are invincible, but because they are secured in a God who is. 2 Corinthians 5:7 reminds us that we walk faithfully and not sight. This verse articulates a basic principle of the Christian life, that believers are called to live in dependence on God's promises, not merely on what is visible or immediately understandable.

> *Christian leaders are called to stand firm in faith, not because they are invincible, but because they are secured in a God who is.*

The term 'walk' comes from the Greek word 'peripateō' meaning, "to live, conduct one's life"[41] It implies a continuous lifestyle or way of living, and 'by faith' denotes trust in God's character and eternal purposes, even when circumstances are unclear. In contrast, not by sight' suggests that spiritual reality often transcends physical perception. For Christian leaders, this verse serves as a call to lead not by human metrics or certainty, but by obedient trust in God's unseen direction and sovereign plan. Maintaining faith in difficult seasons means choosing trust over fear, obedience over convenience, and hope over despair. It means staying faithful when the outcome is unclear.

Difficult seasons bring unique pressure to leaders as people are looking to them for direction, resources may be stretched thin, emotions run high, and outcomes feel uncertain. During such times, when a leader's beliefs are being tested, they must necessarily become the ones who have to 'believe for everyone else'. This is why leaders must be deeply rooted in their personal faith. You cannot lead others in hope if you are disconnected from your very source of hope.

Further, people must recognize that faith is dependence and genuinely trusting the promises of God. The problem is some almost always construe it as denial. However, having faith does not mean pretending things are fine. It means choosing to believe that God is still working even when things are not as anticipated. It means being honest about the reality yet clinging to the truth of who God is. Romans 4:20-21 describes Abraham's posture stating that, "he staggered not at the promise of God through unbelief; but was strong in faith... being fully persuaded that, what he had promised, he was able also to perform." Even without fulfillment in hand, Abraham kept believing. That is the leadership posture of faith where the leader is not pretending but persisting with a knowing that God will hasten His word to bring it to fruition.

There are myriad ways leaders may maintain faith during the moments of stretching. For instance, as indicated in the prior chapters, stay rooted and grounded in the word of God by allowing it to be a lamp to their feel and a light to their path. (Psalm 119:105). Another way leaders can maintain their faith during tough times is to surround themselves with faith-filled voices. The right voices will fuel faith, but the wrong ones will drain it. Wise leaders stay connected to mentors, spiritual leaders, and encouragers who speak life when they feel empty. It is also important to practice declaring God's promises aloud. Speaking faith builds faith. Servant leaders must learn to declare the truth even when their emotions do not match.

One of the things I have noticed in many churches and even organizations is that leaders who hold onto faith become pillars of strength for their teams, congregations, and communities. Their trust becomes contagious. Their steadiness provides a sense of safety. Their endurance gives others permission to hope again. In Tough Times

Never Last, But Tough People Do, Robert H. Schuller discourages readers from allowing their hurt to shape their future. Instead, he urges them to channel their hopes. That is exactly what faith does, it refuses to let pain write the final chapter. Paul modeled this while he was in prison, during storms and betrayal, he still declared, "I know whom I have believed..." (2 Timothy 1:12) Faithful leadership focuses on trusting God with the outcomes we desire rather than trying to control them. In dark seasons, a leader's greatest testimony may not be what they accomplished, but that they stood, believed, and trusted God when it mattered most.

Criticism and Perseverance

No matter how anointed, strategic, or servant-hearted a leader is, criticism is inevitable. From the moment someone steps into influence, their decisions, character, and even motives are subject to scrutiny. And yet, how a Christian leader responds to criticism is a direct reflection of their spiritual maturity, emotional health, and dependence on God. Leadership requires perseverance, especially in the face of opposition. That perseverance is fueled by purpose.

Galatians 6:9 encourages us to avoid becoming exhausted seeking to walk uprightly because if we are able to endure, we will reap the rewards of our labor. In essence, this should be the cry of the persevering leader: "I will not give up, even when I am misunderstood, mistreated, or misjudged." This cry is underpinned be the reassurance that God is with them. Afterall, we have multiple examples from the Bible of leaders who faced heaving criticism and scrutiny greatest of all was Jesus who was constantly attacked, questioned, and ultimately crucified by those who misunderstood His mission.

> *Harsh criticism often comes when you step into bold vision, and results are not yet visible, and when people feel threatened or left behind.*

One of the most painful things a leader has to endure and still persevere is criticisms that come from those closest to them. Sometimes it helps if a leader can find ways to put it all into perspective. Considering this, harsh criticism often comes when you step into bold vision, and results are not yet visible, and when people feel threatened or left behind. With all of this in mind, Christian leaders must be prepared not just to navigate criticism, but to grow through it without losing their voice, values, or vision.

Jesus was no stranger to public scrutiny. He was called a blasphemer, accused of having a demon, and misunderstood even by His disciples. Yet He responded with silence, when necessary (Isaiah 53:7), truth spoken in love, prayer for His enemies (Luke 23:34), and steadfast focus on His mission. The wise leader knows that not every accusation deserves a reaction. Proverbs 15:1 reminds us, "A soft answer turneth away wrath..." And Proverbs 26:4 teaches, "Answer not a fool according to his folly..." This is where discernment comes in. Some criticism is constructive and should be humbly received. Other criticism is rooted in offense, fear, or projection, and must be released to God.

Perseverance is the grit to stay faithful in dry seasons, dark valleys, and moments of rejection. It is refusing to quit when things do not go as planned, or when people fail to respond as hoped. James 1:12 says, "Blessed is the one who perseveres under trial because, having stood the test, that person will receive the crown of life..." This verse highlights the spiritual reward for enduring hardship with faithfulness. It affirms that perseverance through trials is both evidence of genuine faith and the pathway to receiving the "crown of life," a symbol of eternal reward granted by God to those who remain steadfast under pressure. Persevering leaders keep showing up even when discouraged, stay faithful to the word even when tempted to compromise, continue serving others even when unappreciated and stay submitted to God, not public opinion.

Invariably, a leader must leverage the power of wisdom and discernment in order to successfully weather criticisms. Not all critiques are created equal. Some are constructive; others are projections of personal pain and trauma responses. The discerning leader, suffused by the Spirit, will take the time to examine the source. At times, the one meting out the critique is doing so from a place of unresolved suffering, jealousy, or misunderstanding. Yet, even then, the maturing leader must pause long enough to ask the Holy Spirit a difficult but transformational question: "Is there truth in this?" That question does not weaken a leader, it refines them by shifting the response from reaction to reflection.

One of the most sobering yet empowering verses in Scripture regarding critique and correction is found in Proverbs 9:8-9 which states, "Reprove not a scorner, lest he hate thee: rebuke a wise man, and he will love thee. Give instruction to a wise man, and he will be yet wiser: teach a just man, and he will increase in learning." This passage establishes a powerful distinction between the foolish and the wise, not in how they speak, but in how they receive correction. The scorner, a proud unteachable person, rejects critique and becomes bitter. But the *wise* embrace it and grow stronger. The Hebrew word for *wise* here, 'ḥākām', refers to both intellectual acumen and moral and spiritual insight. In essence, a sincerely wise leader understands that correction, even when uncomfortable, is a tool for elevation.

Also, maintaining perspective is indispensable to effective and operative leadership, guiding a leader through tempestuous waters. Criticism, often seen as an attack, can actually confirm that you are leading boldly and challenging norms. If you are impacting others, resistance is inevitable. Jesus Christ, the perfect leader, faced relentless criticism, misunderstanding, false accusations, and questioning even from those closest to Him. Even then, He remained firm in His identity and assignment. Leaders today must adopt this same resolve.

The dynamic nature of leadership demands continual calibration, as John Maxwell states in his book, LeaderShift, today's best will not meet tomorrow's challenges. Leadership is never static; it is a perpetual process of learning and adapting to remain effective. This growth often comes with friction, requiring leaders to not just handle pressure but convert it into spiritual growth. The Apostle Paul reinforces this in Romans 5:3-4 where he states, "We glory in tribulations also: knowing that tribulation worketh patience; and patience, experience; and experience, hope." Each layer of pressure refines a leader's character, deepening their sanctification and solidifying an unshakeable hope.

Every leader face criticism, but spiritual maturity lies in the Spirit-led response. Christian leadership calls for a delicate yet potent duality; profound tenderness (compassion, humility) coupled with steadfast toughness (conviction, courage). This balance, sustained by resilience, allows leaders to endure adversity without compromising core values. The mature leader views criticism and reproach as a classroom. They see it as an opportunity for introspection, self-assessment, and growth. By espousing this, leaders are continually conformed into the image of Christ, simultaneously demonstrating this transformative path to others.

PART THREE:

MULTIPLYING IMPACT AND PROTECTING LEGACY

"Legacy is not what you leave behind, but who you send forward."

—Shauna-kaye Brown

CHAPTER 6

NAVIGATING THE TRAPS AND PITFALLS

The Burden of Influence

"With great power comes great responsibility."

– Voltaire

This is a quote popularized by Spider-Man comics, but originally attributed to 18th-century French philosopher Voltaire. Though modern pop culture helped this phrase gain traction, its origins point back to philosophical and even biblical principles. The quote aligns powerfully with the spiritual weight Christian leaders carry. Influence is not just a benefit, it is a responsibility that demands integrity and discernment. Luke 12:48 tells us, "For unto whomsoever much is given, of him shall be much required: and to whom men have committed much, of him they will ask the more." **Kingdom influence is largely about stewardship, a burden that should lead us to**

depend more deeply on God. Influence when entrusted to a Christian leader, is not just about guiding others, it is about stewarding souls. It is both a privilege and a pressure, both a platform and a potential pitfall.

Influence is subtle and it grows as people begin to trust your voice, follow your lead, and shape their decisions around your example. But what happens when that influence is mishandled? We have seen it far too often where gifted leaders were brought down not by a lack of vision but by a lack of vigilance. In the wrong hands, influence becomes a weapon. In the hands of a surrendered leader, it becomes a tool for transformation. Many organizations are run by leaders who profess God but lead from a place of 'self'. They may be powerful in their eyes and to those who put them in charge, but they do not have the backing of heaven so long as they fail to steward their influence correctly.

> *Influence is subtle and it grows as people begin to trust your voice, follow your lead, and shape their decisions around your example.*

One sobering example of this is found in the life of King Saul. Anointed by God, positioned by grace, Saul began well. But over time, influence became an idol. In 1

Samuel 15, Saul disobeys God's direct command. When confronted by the prophet Samuel, his reasoning is chilling: "I feared the people, and obeyed their voice." Here lies a powerful lesson. Saul was called to influence people, but instead, he was influenced by them. He let his fear of man outweigh his fear of God. His fall reminds us that the burden of influence requires more than charisma, it demands obedience, integrity, and meekness.

Consider also James 3:1, which cautions, "My brethren, be not many masters, knowing that we shall receive the greater condemnation." This scripture reveals the gravity of leadership. Those who teach, lead, and influence others will be held to a higher standard. Why? Because when you carry influence, your choices echo beyond your own life. Influence multiplies impact, for better or for worse.

This chapter explores the internal and external tensions leaders face when carrying the weight of influence. It examines the temptations of power, the erosion caused by pride, the fragility of moral integrity, and the danger of isolation. Also, it offers practical and spiritual safeguards for leaders who want to finish well and influence wisely. You will be challenged to look inward, to test your motives, and to realign your influence under the Lordship of Christ. Because in the Kingdom, leadership is not about how many follow you, it is about how faithfully you follow Him and how well you treat His children.

Temptation of Power and Authority

One of the greatest dangers in Christian leadership is the enticement to misuse power and authority. Leaders must be careful not to mismanage and manipulate their sphere of influence. If influence is not stewarded with humility, it becomes intoxication. What begins as service can quietly turn into control. What starts in surrender can drift into self-exaltation. This is not a new concept but has existed since time immemorial and is the reason so many leaders fall, not from incompetence, but from unchecked ambition.

> *Power can be a seductive enemy to a Christian leader.*

Earlier, the matter of life balance was addressed, now we are concerned with the balance of power and authority. Power can be a seductive enemy to a Christian leader. Importantly, power, by itself, is not evil. In fact, God gives His leaders spiritual authority to lead boldly and protect the flock. In Luke 10:19, He expressly states that He has given us power to trample upon the wiles of the enemy. However, the danger comes when leaders forget who gave them that authority and start operating like they own it. Oh, how detrimental this is to leadership success.

In both the spiritual and the secular world, many leaders abuse their zone of power through manipulative tactics. Such leaders are usually insecure and believe they have little or no impact unless they exert their power through manipulation. They usually go to great lengths to make sure their presence is felt, often to the detriment of their leadership impact. The major issue with this is most leaders realize the damage they are causing when it is already too late. Markus Zehentner and Claudia Schwinghammer contend that, "manipulative bosses can create a toxic work environment, negatively impacting employee morale, productivity, and mental health."[42] It is not enough to dissuade leaders from abuse of power and manipulation, those under their care should also be cautioned and educated to recognize these behaviors. This will help them to navigate and manage effectively.

In Deuteronomy 8:17-18, God warns His people, "You may say to yourself, 'My power and the strength of my hands have produced this wealth for me.' But remember the Lord your God, for it is He who gives you the ability to produce wealth." Leaders who stop acknowledging God as their source often begin to build platforms instead of people, protect their position instead of their integrity, and lead from self-importance instead of service. However, they need to recognize that power without submission is dangerous. To be sustainable, spiritual authority must remain under God's authority. The moment a leader believes they are above correction, accountability, or Scripture, they are on perilous ground.

> *Leaders who stop acknowledging God as their source often begin to build platforms instead of people, protect their position instead of their integrity, and lead from self-importance instead of service.*

Consider King Saul for instance, 1 Samuel 15 shows us where he misused his authority, disobeyed God, and lost everything in the process. King Uzziah became proud in strength and was struck with leprosy for overstepping his role. However, we see from 2 Chronicles 26 that he was prematurely inducted into the seat of king which could have contributed to his lack of discernment in leadership. Isn't that what happening to a lot of our leaders? They either go into leadership of their own accord or they inherit a role for which they were not prepared. This is a sure way to fall into the trap of poor leadership. Authority in the Kingdom is about is about servanthood, not dominance.

The good thing about a leader's ability to avert the traps and pitfalls of power and authority is that there are usually signs that they are becoming a temptation. For instance, as a leader, if you often resist correction, feedback, or seek more to control rather than to empower, there may be evidence of an unhealthy power dynamic. If you demand loyalty but struggle to give trust or use 'God told me, 'To end conversations, there is again an over-exertion of authority. Finally, if you increasingly rely on title instead of testimony, there your reference point is one of power rather than God's truth about overcoming by the power of your testimony. These red flags often indicate that influence has become identity which is a dangerous shift that leads to spiritual and relational consequences.

Jesus flipped the script on authority when He indicated in Matthew 20:25-28 that anyone who wanted to become great must start with servanthood. Bear in mind that Jesus had all authority, yet He washed feet and healed the sick and the unclean. He rode into Jerusalem on a donkey, not a warhorse which would not have been unforeseeable at the time. He rebuked religious pride and modeled what it meant to lead with humility instead of entitlement. I submit that any leader who follows Christ must follow this counter-cultural model of power Authority that submits, power that serves and influence that lifts other up.

> *To guard their heart against the power and authority trap, leaders must stay accountable by having qualified accountability partners that speak into your lives, even when it is uncomfortable.*

To guard their heart against the power and authority trap, leaders must stay accountable by having qualified accountability partners that speak into your lives, even when it is uncomfortable. They must also remain steadfast in God's word and let Scripture search your motives daily. It is of utmost importance that leaders also stay in the service of others by doing the unseen, unglamorous tasks like praying behind the scenes. Wise leaders also stay Spirit-dependent. The moment a leader feels they can 'do this without God,' they are in danger. Finally, leaders must remain rooted in identity, not position. They must remain cognizant of who they are in Christ without needing applause, titles, or influence to prove it. In The Spirit of Leadership, Dr. Myles Munroe warns that leadership is about service, not control. Therefore, the spirit of leadership is diametrically opposed to the attitude of power. Kingdom leadership begins where ego ends.

In summary, leaders mut recognize that power is a tool, not an identity. When stewarded with humility and submission, it can bring healing, growth, and transformation. But when mishandled, it can bring destruction to both the leader and the people they serve. Leaders must also remember that they do not hold the power, God does. The only way to carry it well is to carry it with humility, fear of the Lord, and a servant's heart.

Moral and Ethical Failures

Moral and ethical failures have left deep scars in the body of Christ. The fall of prominent leaders, whether through sexual sin, financial dishonesty, abuse of power, or compromised character, has caused public scandals, private devastation, and spiritual confusion for countless followers. But failure does not begin with a single act. It often begins with compromised conviction over time. As Christian leaders, we must not only grieve these failures, but we must also understand them, guard against them, and cultivate lifestyles of ongoing integrity. Proverbs 4:23 warn us to ensure our heart is diligently protected because everything about our lives emanates from it. Understand that the fall never starts on the stage, it starts in the heart.

How we avert moral and ethical failures is to understand their roots. Moral and ethical collapses rarely happen overnight. They are the result of ignored warning signs and internal erosion. Some common causes are discussed throughout this chapter. Such include lack of accountability, entitlement, fatigue, pride, gradual compromise, and lack of boundaries. The moment a leader believes 'the rules don't apply to me,' they are already on dangerous ground.

Christian ethics seeks to identify and systematize moral principles enabling leaders to act with consistency, integrity, and fidelity to the gospel in all areas of influence.

A classic example is found in 2 Samuel 11 where David, a man after God's heart, gave in to lust, deception, and murder. Note that David's failure did not start with Bathsheba, it started when he stayed home from battle, out of position. In Judges 16, we see where Samson compromised repeatedly and ultimately lost his strength and vision. In Acts 5, Ananias and Sapphira lied about money in the early church, and it cost them their lives. The message is clear, God takes leadership integrity seriously, because leadership has influence, and influence carries responsibility. In the life of a Christian leader, ethics is more than policies and rules. Christian ethics seeks to identify and systematize moral principles enabling leaders to act with consistency, integrity, and fidelity to the gospel in all areas of influence. Christian ethics are a reflection of a leader's inner life, what they value when no one is looking.

Ethical leaders keep their word, even when it is inconvenient. They refuse to manipulate people for personal gain, handle finances with transparency and stewardship, establish healthy boundaries in relationships, and exercise self-discipline even when another way seems inviting. Maybe this is the reason "many highly gifted leaders have stopped far short of their potential because they were not willing to pay the price."[43] Instead, they forego morally sound avenues and choose options that compromise their integrity because they appear more alluring. However, leaders must recognize that moral excellence matters more than giftedness, and this often means being disciplined in your leadership. Meanwhile, being ethical means avoiding the shortcuts even when they seem enticing. To be morally and ethically sound, a leader must be deliberate in their actions and always seek to align with God's will.

When a Christian leader falls prey to unethical and immoral conduct, they break individuals' trust in their leadership. They also dishonor the name of Christ causing followers to abandon their faith and future leaders to give in to hesitation and cynicism. Highlighting these pitfalls is not to shame leaders, but to emphasize the weight of responsibility carried by those in spiritual authority. James 3:1 presents a sober warning to those aspiring to teach or lead in the Church. James cautions that teachers will be held to a stricter judgment because their influence shapes minds, hearts, and spiritual direction. Teaching God's word is not merely a position of honor but one of profound responsibility, requiring both doctrinal accuracy and personal integrity. In short, leadership multiplies impact and accountability.

To prevent moral failure, leaders have a responsibility to hold themselves and others in their care accountable and remain teachable as learning is a lifelong journey. Of course, they should also practice daily intimacy with God because sin loses power when we stay in His presence. The remarkable thing about our God is He is forgiving and understanding. Though failure is serious, it is not final. Leaders who fall are not beyond God's reach. Restoration is possible, but it must be rooted in repentance, accountability, and time. After his fall, David asked God to make his heart pure again and give him a spirit that is aligned with Him. The forgiving and understanding God we serve does not disqualify. However, he does call for humility and honesty before Him. Moral and ethical failure does not happen because someone was a bad leader, it happens when good leaders stop guarding their heart, habits, and holiness. The calling of Christian leadership is sacred. It must be protected through daily surrender and intentional integrity. The Church does not need perfect leaders, it needs repentant, accountable, and Holy Spirit led ones.

Pride and Fame

Pride has been referenced several times through this book and that is perhaps because of all the leadership pitfalls, it is the most deceptive. This verse draws a clear line in the spiritual sand. God actively opposes those who exalt themselves, rely on their own strength, and refuse correction. In contrast, He lavishly gives grace to those who recognize their need for Him, walk in submission, and depend on His mercy. Pride invites resistance while humility invites divine help. Pride and the pursuit of fame have subtly infiltrated Christian leadership culture. In an age of platforms, followers, and personal branding, it is easier than ever for leaders to seek influence over intimacy, applause over anointing, and visibility over obedience. As a Christian leader with a platform, I am constantly reminded of the insidious nature of pride and fame, and I am constantly asking God to shield me.

> *Pride always set leaders on a collision course with the discipline of God.*

What is the anatomy of pride in leadership? The truth is, she does not always look arrogant. Sometimes, pride appears as unwillingness to be corrected and a need to always be right. Other times, leaders give in to constant evaluation of their ministry against others and take credit for what only God can do. One of the first known sins in the Bible is the demise of Lucifer and we know the premise of it. Isaiah 14:13-14 confirms that Lucifer fell because of pride. He sought to lift himself up to the position of God. Pride always set leaders on a collision course with the discipline of God.

Zehentner and Schwinghammer in "Breaking Free from Toxic Leadership" contend that, "individuals who excel in self-promotion, may ascend to leadership positions despite lacking the necessary competencies to be truly effective leaders." Such leaders usually foster a toxic work environment and intensify the challenge of nurturing a collaborative and positive work culture.[44] Pride does not just affect the leaders; it affects their environment.

> *Many leaders embark on their leadership journey with pure intentions, genuinely called by God, marked by surrender, brokenness, and a desire to serve.*

Fame is enticing because it offers what feels like success, visibility, praise, admiration, influence. However, without accountability it is dangerous. Fame feeds ego, isolates leaders, and often turns servants into celebrities. Jesus, our ultimate leadership maven never pursued fame. In fact, He often told people *not* to talk about His miracles. He often withdrew from crowds, avoided publicity, and chose the path of obscurity until it was time to fulfill His mission. Spiritual authority is built in the private places of surrender and obedience, not public platforms as many are inclined to establish today. In his book 'In the Name of Jesus', Henri Nouwen tells us that the lure of significance, power and status can only be overcome by prioritizing prayer and community.

Many leaders embark on their leadership journey with pure intentions, genuinely called by God, marked by surrender, brokenness, and a desire to serve. However, over time, as influence expands and recognition intensifies, some shift their focus from people to performance. They begin to prioritize numbers over souls and rely more on applause than on anointing. This drift can lead to diminished teachability, increased defensiveness, and a growing obsession with personal branding, often at the expense of spiritual authenticity. In leaders overtaken by pride and the lure of fame, we witness a subtle but dangerous transition from humble beginnings to ego-driven leadership. Tragically, this gradual shift from calling to celebrity often goes unnoticed until it culminates in burnout, disillusionment, or even collapse.

The antidote to pride and fame is a daily return to humility. As encouraged by Matthew 6:4, leaders need to normalize serving in secret allowing God to reward what no one sees. They must understand that pride thrives in denial and therefore they should seek always to walk in the light where egoism diminishes. Leaders should also intentionally counter comparison by honoring others and endeavor to spend time with people who are unimpressed by their title. They should never lose sight of the finished work on the cross remembering that exist to lift up Jesus, not themselves.

Pride is both a personal sin and a leadership liability. It hardens hearts, blinds vision, and corrupts motives. Fame, when pursued, often becomes a substitute for actual fruit.

Unfortunately, we live in a society that glorifies these traps of good leadership. But God does not elevate leaders to make them famous, He raises them to make Him known. The leaders who leave the deepest legacy are not those who were most visible, but those who were most surrendered.

Isolation and Lack of Support

It is extremely dangerous for a leader to find themself alone whether physically, emotionally, spiritually, or relationally. This is one of the major traps on a leader's trajectory. It is well established that leadership often comes with heavy responsibilities, immense pressure, and ongoing expectations, but when it is carried in isolation, it becomes heavy enough to crush. Also, isolation is not always chosen and that is probably when it is most risky. It can be insidious developing subtly out of factors such as the fear of being misunderstood, because the leader feels 'no one else gets it' or the leader is nursing relational wounds or recovering from a betrayal. Isolation may also result from overwork and burnout or from a pedestal-based leadership culture that separates leaders from their people.

However, leaders must understand that isolation is a setup for certain ruins and therefore take intentional steps to avert it. Ecclesiastes 4:9-10 reminds us that, "two are better than one... For if they fall, the one will lift up his fellow: but woe to him that is alone when he falleth." Here, we see the inherent value of partnership and mutual support in human relationships. The statement "two are better than one" reflects a perceptive principle, collaboration yields greater fruit than solitary effort especially where labor is involved. The part that speaks about what happens if they fall highlights the necessity of accountability and emotional support during moments of failure or hardship.

Conversely, for the person who finds themself secluded, there is certainty of a struggle in recovery. It serves as a sobering reminder that self-sufficiency is not a biblical leadership model. Instead, the word of God advocates for interdependence, where leaders surround themselves with others who can offer encouragement, correction, and strength. In this context, the passage reinforces the importance of spiritual community, mentorship, and shared responsibility for enduring life's challenges and fulfilling one's calling.

Many leaders believe the lie that strength means handling it alone even when the Bible give use myriad examples of the converse. As previously established, some of the strongest leaders in Scripture never led in isolation. Moses had support from Aaron, Hur, and he also had

Jethro's counsel. David had Jonathan, Nathan, and his mighty men. Paul traveled with Barnabas, Silas, Luke, Timothy, and others and most significant of all, Jesus surrounded Himself with the 'twelve' and still invited three into deeper connection, namely, Peter, James, and John. If the Son of God did not lead alone, why should we think it is wise to take this approach?

> *Isolation weakens a leader because usually when they extricate themselves from others, they stop being vulnerable, stop receiving correction, and sometimes even lose perspective.*

In 'Mentoring Leaders', Carson Pue writes, "A leader without support is a leader in danger."[45] Still, every so often you see some church leaders whose positions as head of the ministry are already solidified and yet, they will not allow others to support them. They are in fact leading from a place of insecurity where vision is absent and self-preservation seems to take preeminence over discernment. They hold on to the charge of the pulpit so tightly as if their lives depend on it and unfortunately, for some, it does cost them their life. The reality is, isolation weakens a leader because usually when they extricate themselves from others, they stop being vulnerable, stop receiving correction, and sometimes even lose perspective as to the will of God.

Typically, the danger intensifies when the isolated leader becomes emotionally worn and starts to nurture secret struggles. Soon they may find themself leading a double life showing up one way publicly and another privately without knowing how to manage this due to lack of support. According to Zehentner and Schwinghammer, "a solid support network can provide emotional and practical assistance, helping you to navigate the complexities of your situation."[46] What leaders must realize is that unseen struggle becomes unaddressed sin. What can be healed in community often festers in isolation.

Still, one should not ignore the plethora of reasons leaders may select to withdraw. Understanding the 'why' behind isolation can help leaders recognize and reverse it. Some common reasons leaders include fear of judgment or appearing weak, shame from past mistakes, bitterness stemming from betrayal, busyness that crowds out relationships, and pride or hyper-independence. However, the cost of staying hidden is always greater than the pain of being seen. The Bible does not set any expectation for leaders to be great, they simply need to work towards leading as Jesus did, with compassion, integrity, and unconditional love. Leadership wins when leaders realize they are human and therefore fallible beings who are not expected to go on the course alone.

The fact that isolation is detrimental does not mean leaders should immerse themselves in random communities without exercising discernment. God never designed leaders to carry the weight of ministry or influence alone but in seeking community, it is imperative that they seek out godly support systems. A staunch support system might include spiritual mentors or overseers, therapists or counselors, trusted peers in ministry, prayer partners and intercessors, and healthy spouse or family dynamics.

These relationships do not just 'check in' to see how you are coping, they check your blind spots, your burnout level, your heart posture. They are careful not to idolize your position as they care for your person. This approach is buttressed by scripture. Hebrews 10:24-25 calls us to encourage one another daily, especially as the spiritual battle intensifies. Isolation dulls discernment while community sharpens it. With this in mind, it is important to create a culture where leaders do not feel the need to hide. As fellow believers, it is not enough to tell leaders 'Do not isolate,' we must create environments where they feel safe to be human. This means:

A. Normalizing therapy, sabbaticals, and spiritual care

B. Releasing leaders from perfectionism

C. Inviting honesty in staff and leadership circles

D. Encouraging rest without guilt, and

E. Cultivating safe, judgment-free zones for confession and healing

Restored leaders are more powerful than burnt-out leaders pretending to be okay. Isolation is not strength; it is a setup for spiritual vulnerability. In the same breath, support is not weakness, it is a strategy for longevity. The leaders who finish well are not those who carried it all alone, but those who walked with others, leaned on God, and stayed honest about their humanity. Do not lead alone. Do not suffer in silence. Jesus did not take that approach, and you should not have to do it either.

Envy and People-Pleasing

While power, pride, and isolation are visible hazards, envy and people-pleasing operate in the shadows, quietly eroding a leader's joy, authenticity, and effectiveness. Envy whispers lies like, 'You are not enough unless you are like them.' People-pleasing echoes, 'You are only as valuable as their approval.' Together, these traps drive leaders to compete instead of collaborating, mimic instead of minister, and perform instead of lead. These traps may not always make headlines like scandal or pride, but they do incredible damage to a leader's soul, decisions, and direction. They are sins of the heart that can twist calling into competition and stewardship into self-preservation. James 3:14-16 expresses the poison of envy quite plainly stating, "But if you have bitter envy and selfish ambition in your heart, do not boast about it or deny the truth. Such 'wisdom' does not come down from heaven but is earthly, unspiritual, demonic." The scripture offers a piercing diagnosis of envy and selfish ambition. It warns that when these attitudes take root in the heart, they distort the truth and lead to deception. James makes it clear that this kind of 'wisdom' does not come from God. Instead, it is earthly and therefore limited to worldly thinking, unspiritual and thus void of the Spirit, and demonic which is aligned with the enemy's nature. The result? Confusion, disorder, and toxic environments and communities.

> *Envy is not a mere character flaw; it is a gateway to disorder and every evil work.*

Envy is not a mere character flaw; it is a gateway to disorder and every evil work. It robs leaders of gratitude and distort their calling as they seek to be like others. Leaders who begin comparing their reach, recognition, or results with others open themselves to bitterness, resentment, and rivalry. Envy corrupts motivation, making ministry a competition instead of calling. Rick Warren posits that, "you cannot fulfill

God's purpose for your life if you envy the lives of others."47 God created us as original with unique paths to the fulfillment of His purpose, envying others runs contrary to the plan of God. To attempt to be what you were not created to be is a recipe for failure and frustration.

> *Envy is really a thief who blinds leaders to what God has entrusted them with by keeping their eyes glued to someone else's assignment.*

Envy is really a thief who blinds leaders to what God has entrusted them with by keeping their eyes glued to someone else's assignment. In 1 Samuel 18:7-9, we see where Saul, though chosen and anointed, could not celebrate David's victories. His jealousy consumed him, driving him into insecurity, rage, and destruction. According to Matthew Henry in a Bible commentary, every society is plagued by envy which comes from the devil and destroys from within. Proverbs 14:40 tell us when you hear is at peace, it gives your body its life but when one is filled with envy, it deteriorates the bones. Simply put, envy is a sure path to the destruction of the believer.

People-pleasing on the other hand may feel like humility but it is truly rooted in fear. Fear comes in many forms such as the fear of criticism, being misunderstood or the fear of rejection. Warren calls this the 'dark side' of the desire for approval. However, "the Bible warns us not to let the fear of disapproval keep us from doing what we know God wants us to do."[48] This is the essence of Proverbs 29:25 which tells us that our fear of other people is in fact a dangerous trap. This trap is precipitated by the lie that if everyone likes me then I will be happy. It is highly unlikely that every single person will like you, so it is best to seek to please God rather than people.

> *When believers prioritize the need to be liked, they inadvertently accept a leash around their necks preventing necessary hard truths, delaying obedience, and often causing their own demise.*

In Galatians 1:10, Paul wrote that if he was trying to please man he would fail in his assignment of being a servant of Christ. When believers prioritize the need to be liked, they inadvertently accept a leash around their necks preventing necessary hard truths, delaying obedience, and often causing their own demise. Soon, the leader who subscribes to this way of being starts shaping messages for applause, not impact. Not only was King Saul envious but he also did some people-pleasing. In 1 Samuel 15:24, Saul admits that he was afraid of the people and so he gave in to them thus disobeying God's command to destroy the Amalekites. That one sentence explains Saul's downfall. He sacrificed obedience for optics.

ESCAPING THE HIDDEN TRAPS: A CALL TO HEART-CHECK LEADERSHIP

How can a Christian leader become aware of the subtle traps threatening their effectiveness and integrity? It begins with honest self-examination. If you constantly compare your ministry to others, feel resentful when someone else succeeds, or question your worth when others are celebrated, these are not minor flaws. They are signals of envy, a spiritual snare that erodes gratitude and distorts vision. Similarly, when you say "yes" to avoid disapproval, steer clear of confrontation, require applause to feel validated, or shift your message to align with popular culture, you are already entangled in the web of people-pleasing. These behaviors often masquerade as humility or diplomacy, but in reality, they are premised on fear, insecurity, and misplaced identity.

To combat these traps, Christian leaders must make a deliberate shift from public opinion to divine direction. Knowing who you are in Christ, and who you are not, is foundational. Galatians 1:10 asks, "For do I now persuade men, or God? or do I seek to please men? for if I yet pleased men, I should not be the servant of Christ." This sobering reminder reinforces that people-pleasing is incompatible with servanthood. Leaders must cultivate the spiritual maturity to prioritize God's approval over applause, truth over trend, and obedience over status and acceptance. Jesus, the ultimate model, never adjusted His message to gain favor. He offended religious elites and disappointed crowds, yet fulfilled His divine assignment with unyielding clarity. That is the leader's goal, not popularity, but purpose. The right thinking and acting leader must be driven by this same purpose.

> *Christian leaders must reject the seductive lure of being envied or liked and instead root themselves in God-confidence and faithful obedience.*

Envy and people-pleasing are not mere leadership weaknesses; they are spiritual quicksand. Left unchecked, they will consume your confidence, distort your message, and compromise your impact. Christian leaders must reject the seductive lure of being envied or liked and instead root themselves in God-confidence and faithful obedience. Your calling is too sacred to be shaped by someone else's shadow.

Kingdom leadership demands a courage that is both rare and resolute, the courage to stand alone where necessary, to celebrate others with sincerity, and to speak truth with boldness, even when the applause is absent. It also calls for spiritual discernment. In an age saturated with counterfeits, leaders must be vigilant against deceptive ideologies that cloak themselves in light but contradict the very heart of God's Word.

We are witnessing an increasing fusion of New Age philosophies, such as the law of attraction, energy alignment, and creative visualization, with biblical language. This is not harmless syncretism; it is a dangerous distortion. These practices are rooted in self-deification and human-centered power, not in the sovereign will of God. They cannot coexist with the Gospel and will never lead anyone into true communion with the Father. There is only one authorized way to "manifest" anything of eternal value, and that is through alignment with God's principles, by submitting fully to His will, and walking in obedience to His Word.

Romans 12:2 exhorts us, "And be not conformed to this world: but be ye transformed by the renewing of your mind, that ye may prove what is that good, and acceptable, and perfect, will of God." Here we have a powerful framework for Christian leadership. It begins with a clear prohibition: "Be not conformed to this world." The Greek word for 'conformed' is syschēmatizō, meaning to fashion or shape oneself after another pattern. Paul is warning against adopting the values, philosophies, and behaviors of the world system, which is under the sway of sin and self-interest. This is especially pertinent to Kingdom leaders, who are constantly under pressure to conform to secular standards of success, influence, and popularity.

Instead of conforming, Paul calls believers to "be transformed." The Greek term here is metamorphoō, from which we get the English word 'metamorphosis.' This denotes a complete, inward change that reveals itself outwardly, much like a caterpillar becoming a butterfly. The transformation Paul refers to is not superficial or cosmetic; it is deep, ongoing, and spiritual in nature. And how does this transformation occur? "By the renewing of your mind." The renewal Paul speaks of involves a radical reprogramming of our thoughts, perspectives, and desires through the fact of God's Word and the sanctifying work of the Holy Spirit. This is not a one-time event, but a daily process of exchanging worldly thoughts for Kingdom truth.

The purpose of this transformation is "that ye may prove what is that good, and acceptable, and perfect, will of God." To prove here means to discern, test, and affirm. Only a renewed mind can properly understand and walk in God's will. For leaders, this verse is non-negotiable. Leaders who conform to cultural trends may gain applause, but they will miss God's intention. Leaders who undergo transformation through God's principles and expectations become capable of discerning and executing His will with clarity, maturity, and conviction.

Kingdom leaders, therefore, are not to imitate the fleeting patterns of this world but to embody the eternal mind and message of Christ. Transformation is not achieved through mystical techniques, manifestation rituals, or self-empowerment mantras like affirmations, it is birthed through spiritual surrender and the daily renewing of the inner man with the spoken word of God encapsulated in scripture. For instance, "I have a Spirit of power and of love and of a sound mind," is an effective declaration over your life given to us by God in 2 Timothy 1:7.

As we work to raise a generation of servant-hearted, Spirit-led leaders, we must begin by purging every compromise that erodes character and misaligns vision. We must reject the seductive pull of worldly shortcuts and reclaim the sacred call to lead with focus, integrity, and allegiance to God's truth. It is only from that place of clarity and consecration that leaders can rise for eternity.

CHAPTER 7

CREATING LEGACY

Identifying and Empowering Future Leaders for Lasting Impact

"Success is when I add value to myself.
Significance is when I add value to others."

– Dr. John C. Maxwell

Maxwell's point of view pierces straight to the heart of legacy. Leadership that ends with self, no matter how accomplished, is vastly limited as well as limiting. Alternatively, leadership that pours into others, that multiplies through mentoring and development, becomes eternal in its impact. In the Kingdom of God, this is good strategy aligned with heavenly order which is being carried out in the earth. This is quite appropriate and pleasing to God as it is our domain of power and authority.

Leadership is more about creating leaders and less concerned with creating a following. Jesus Himself exemplified this when He spent three years investing deeply in twelve disciples, not for applause, but for continuity. He was intentional in His training, personal in His approach, and strategic in His release. His ministry did not end at the cross. It exploded through those He equipped to carry it forward. This should be the goal of every leader as they assume their responsibility.

> *Leadership is more about creating leaders and less concerned with creating a following.*

A powerful modern-day example of this principle is Dr. Myles Munroe. Known for his profound teachings on purpose and leadership, Dr. Munroe built more than a platform, he built people. Through the work of the Bahamas Faith Ministries and his global mentorship efforts, he raised up countless leaders, many of whom are still carrying the weight of transformational leadership long after his passing. His teachings on kingdom purpose, identity, and leadership were not confined to conference rooms or pulpits. They were embedded into the lives of the men and women he personally discipled. What sets Dr.

Munroe apart was not only his depth of knowledge, but his commitment to duplication. He believed that great leadership was not proven by how many followed you, but by how many you empowered to lead. And that belief shaped a legacy that is still unfolding today.

This chapter challenges every leader to rethink what it means to finish well. It is not enough to lead faithfully in your lifetime. You must identify, invest in, and empower those who will carry the torch long after you are gone. It means letting go of personal ego to make room for emerging voices. It means trading moments of spotlight for decades of impact. And it means pouring into others without needing to be praised for doing so. Here, you are invited to reflect on how you are shaping the next generation, not just with your words, but with your presence, your example, and your intentionality. Because in the end, legacy is not measured by 'what' you leave behind. It is measured by 'who' you leave behind. And the greatest leaders are not remembered for how they stood alone, but for how they raised others to stand after them.

A Lifelong Calling

Christian leadership transcends what you accomplish during your lifetime. It is concerned with an enduring calling to lead as Jesus did. Legacy goes beyond fame, fortune, or fanfare. In the Kingdom of God, legacy is defined by faithfulness, impact, and multiplication through nurturing others. As Ryan Franklin contends, "investing in the development of others is one of the most important jobs of an effective leader."[49] A leader must prioritize leaving behind more than buildings and a good name. **They should endeavor always to carry out the great Commission that Matthew 28:19-20 speaks of, that is, making disciples of all nations.**

> *leadership legacy begins the day you say 'yes 'to God's call, and it is built one obedient step at a time.*

Legacy in leadership is not about passing down a testimony. Psalm 145:4 reminds us that each generation is called to proclaim God's greatness to the next. That means our leadership should not end with impact, but with impartation. We do not just model excellence, but we declare the mighty acts of God so that those coming after us walk in deeper faith and not simply better systems. True spiritual leadership ensures that the next generation does not have to guess Who God is, they will know, because we told them. Indeed, legacy is about passing on what God has deposited in you, so that others can carry it forward with honesty, and spiritual momentum.

The first step a leader should seek to take is to answer the question, why am I here? Or as Rick Warrant puts it, "what on earth am I here for?"[50] Warren answers this, and others of the most probing questions human beings have throughout their lifetime. The ultimate approach is to begin with understanding what you came here to do. Maybe if more leaders were aware of why they were born in the first place, it would keep them on track with their divine assignment.

Leadership legacy begins the day you say 'yes 'to God's call, and it is built one obedient step at a time. In The Christian Leader Blueprint, Ryan Franklin writes, "developing others is essential to the leader who wants to lead an organization with a lasting legacy."[51] This principle speaks to the heart of transformational leadership and does not only apply to organizations. A leader's impact is measured by what they build as well as who they build. When leaders intentionally mentor, equip, and release others into purpose, they extend the reach of their calling beyond their own lifetime. Jesus demonstrated this by pouring into His disciples, entrusting them with the message of the Gospel. Developing others ensures that the vision continues long after the original leader has finished their course. That is how legacy is formed, through people.

Here is a profound truth to consider, your life is the message. As Paul expressed to the Corinthians, their lives were the living proof of his ministry, etched on his heart and visible for all to see. **A lifelong calling means understanding that you are the message.** Your choices, your humility, your faithfulness in private and public moments, they preach louder than your sermons ever could.

> *Legacy is about doing the right things with obedience, consistency, and heart.*

Leaders who walk with Christ over the long-haul build credibility through consistency and teach with authenticity and grace. These are the kinds of leaders who inspire for more than just one season. In fact, they disciple well beyond their natural life as their impact usually lives on, like Dr. Myles Munroe who passed away in the year 2014. His legacy speaks now more than ever before. He truly embodied the legacy leader we are talking about here.

In today's culture of short attention spans and fast fame, finishing well is a rare but radical act. Leaders who endure through myriad adversities and transition with their hearts still soft and their faith still strong, leave a powerful legacy that echoes for decades. Hebrews 12:1-2 calls us to run with endurance, looking to Jesus. Legacy is about long obedience in the same direction. It focuses on keeping your soul healthy and your vision unending. You may never see the full fruit of your labor. But legacy-minded leaders trust that God finishes what they start. The goal of Christian leadership is to point others to the One who never changes.

> *A leader's impact is measured by what they build as well as who they build.*

Legacy is about doing the right things with obedience, consistency, and heart. Leaders who understand that their calling spans a lifetime will finish well and inspire others to do the same. These are the caliber of leaders who are perhaps more inclined to hear, "Well done, thou good and faithful servant." (Matthew 25:21).

The Power of Duplication

Years ago, I sat in a class led by Dr. Demetrius Robinson, the lead pastor of One God Ministry based out of Milwaukee, Wisconsin, USA. During that session, he said something so simple, yet so deeply profound, it has never left me. Dr. Robinson said, "God created human beings for multiplication." At the time, I heard it as a spiritual principle. But as the years passed and my journey in leadership deepened, I came to realize the weight of that statement. Dr. Robinson was not just talking about biological reproduction, he was talking about legacy. About impact. About the divine design hardwired into every believer, especially those called to lead. That one sentence by Dr. Robinson shaped how I see my role as a leader, not to hoard influence but to multiply it. Not to be the end, but a conduit. Christian leadership, at its core, is about creating disciples who go on to disciple others. That is multiplication and legacy, and it is what I pray to live out every day.

> *God's plan was not intended for our influence to end with us. He designed us to pour into others, to multiply vision, character, and calling.*

God's plan was not intended for our influence to end with us. He designed us to pour into others, to multiply vision, character, and calling. This is the reason leadership in the Kingdom cannot be self-centered. It must be generational and reproductive. It must leave fruit that remains. John 15:16 solidifies this perspective that God favors multiplication and duplication. In the scripture, Jesus reminds His disciples that their calling was not initiated by them but by Him. The phrase "you did not choose me, but I chose you" underscores His divine initiative and election, a sovereign call which precedes human response. The word 'ordained' comes from the Greek word, 'tithēmi' which means, "to be placed or put, to set, appoint decide, make."[52] It implies a purposeful placement.

Jesus intentionally positioned His followers for mission. Their purpose? To "go and bring forth fruit," a metaphor for producing lasting spiritual outcomes, such as transformed lives, godly character, and effective ministry. The phrase "fruit should remain" points to eternal impact, not temporary success. Finally, the promise, "whatsoever ye shall ask...in my name" ties fruitfulness to prayerful dependence. It serves as a guarantee of provision when aligned with God's purpose. Fundamentally, John 15:16 teaches that Christian leadership and discipleship are the result of God's choosing, aimed at producing enduring spiritual fruit, empowered by prayer and alignment with Christ's name and mission.

As referenced in chapter four, though Jesus ministered to multitudes, He invested deeply in twelve, and even more intimately, in three. His strategy was core development, he did not focus on crowds. In *Jesus on Leadership*, Wilkes notes that Jesus' goal was never to lead a movement by Himself. His aim was to train followers who would one day do greater works than He did during His earthly travail. When leaders shift from merely producing outcomes to producing others, the Kingdom expands exponentially. So, what does duplication look like in leadership? This encompasses the use of channels such as mentorship, coaching and feedback, modeling, delegation with development, and empowerment and release. It is important for leaders to create safe, honest conversations that help emerging leaders grow in clarity, character, and capacity. Also of import, Christian leaders should prioritize building intentional relationships where wisdom and lived experiences are transferred over time. They should foster environments that allow others to watch their rhythms, decision-making, spiritual life, and leadership under pressure.

> *It is important for leaders to create safe, honest conversations that help emerging leaders grow in clarity, character, and capacity.*

Some leaders struggle with duplication because of insecurity, control issues, unhealed wounds, and lack of intentionality among other hindrances. Sadly, leaders who do not duplicate themselves eventually become single points of failure. When they burn out, retire, or leave, the ministry or movement dies with them. Hence, multiplying leaders are not optional for legacy-minded leadership. We have many points of references from the Bible. For instance, in 2 Kings 2, we see a significant transition of prophetic leadership from Elijah to Elisha. Elisha followed Elijah closely, asked for a double portion, and carried the prophetic mantle forward. Moses mentored Joshua not just in battle strategy but in intimacy with God (Exodus 33:11). Joshua succeeded him in leading Israel. Finally, Paul mentored Timothy, Titus and a host of others. He did not just build churches; he built leaders who became the church. Rather than being transactional, these relationships were deeply personal and intentional.

> *When leaders prioritize duplication, kingdom impact multiplies, ministry becomes sustainable, culture outlives leadership transitions, and communities are built on shared ownership.*

Ultimately, legacy multiplies through both people and programs. Admittedly, events, sermons, and structures are important. However, people are the only legacy that lasts into eternity. When leaders prioritize duplication, kingdom impact multiplies, ministry becomes sustainable, culture outlives leadership transitions, and communities are built on shared ownership. Multiplication is how revival becomes reformation, sustained and scalable. The power of duplication lies in your willingness to pour yourself into others, just as Christ did. Great leaders do more than just leave something behind, they leave someone behind. Someone equipped, empowered, and ready to carry the torch and this is what I do through my company Transform Nations Now LLC. I realize that legacy is not built by keeping people dependent on me, but by training, trusting, and releasing them to run their own race. Duplication ensures that your life's work does not end with you.

The Ministry of Mentorship

The Merriam Webster dictionary defines mentorship as, "influence, guidance, or direction given by a mentor, who is a trusted counselor, guide, tutor, or coach." While biblical mentorship may be construed as the intentional and accountable impartation of truth and character from one generation of leaders to the next, with the goal of multiplication rather than dependency. The latter differs by focusing on deliberate, generational impartation for multiplication, while general mentorship centers on individual guidance and support. When leaders embrace the biblical model, they do more than just create followers, they form future leaders. That is the essence of Kingdom leadership. That is the ministry of mentorship.

A powerful scripture which can be used as a springboard for this conceptualization is 2 Timothy 2:2 which states, "And the things that thou hast heard of me among many witnesses, the same commit thou to faithful men, who shall be able to teach others also." If we were to consider mentorship through the lenses of this verse, we would see that the Apostle Paul placed great emphasis on the intentional and generational transfer of truth, wisdom, and spiritual responsibility. The verse emphasizes that we must value the act of entrusting a sacred deposit to those who will carry it forward with faithfulness and fruitfulness. Here Paul presents us with a four-tier model of multiplication and mentorship:

Paul → Timothy → Faithful men → Others also

This progression presents a biblical blueprint for legacy-minded leadership. Mentorship is not a moment it is a movement. It is God's design for perpetuating sound doctrine, godly character, and Kingdom influence through relational investment. For the ministry of mentorship to be effective, we must understand it at its core. 2 Timothy 2:2 was selected as it represents a biblical model of mentorship across generations. Let's break it down:

A. "The things thou hast heard of me...": This speaks to the content of mentorship, sound doctrine, lived wisdom, and spiritual disciplines. Paul had not just spoken these truths in isolation. Timothy had heard them in the context of community as indicated by, "among many witnesses," showing that mentorship is not hidden, it is accountable and affirmed.

B. "The same commit...": The word 'commit' stems from the Greek word 'paratithēmi' which means "to entrust or deposit for safekeeping". Mentorship, then, is not a casual suggestion but a divine entrusting or a sacred handoff of truth that must be guarded and stewarded with integrity.

C. "To faithful men...": This emphasizes the criteria of mentorship which are faithfulness and giftedness. Mentorship requires discernment. Paul tells Timothy not to teach just anyone, but to identify those who are proven, trustworthy, and teachable. Faithfulness is the soil in which fruitfulness grows.

D. "Who shall be able to teach others also.": This reveals the goal of mentorship which is multiplication. It is not enough for the mentee to receive truth; they must be able to reproduce it in others. The chain of transformation continues as each generation teaches the next.

This Biblical model of mentorship is strategic, spiritually sound, and scalable. It ensures that what begins with one leader does not end with them. Instead, it multiplies across time, culture, and communities. Many leaders today are afraid to intentionally shepherd others according to this model as they are insecure about their position. These are positional leaders who cannot see the negative implication of such a myopic purview on leadership. Unfortunately, countless ministries have ceased to exist after the leader dies because they did not practice intentional multiplication while they lived.

While training can equip a leader for function, only mentorship transforms them for purpose.

From Paul's blueprint, we can see that the true power of Christian leadership is not found in how much a leader can do but how many leaders they can raise, develop, and release. This is the power of duplication and multiplication we have been talking about. Understand that reproducing your values, vision, and spiritual DNA in others, so the mission continues long after you are gone is paramount. That is why the Apostle Paul told Timothy that everything he taught, especially what was affirmed by many reliable witnesses, was to be passed on to trustworthy individuals who would also be able to teach others in turn. Here, Paul is instructing Timothy on how to preserve and pass on sound doctrine. However, while training can equip a leader for function, only mentorship transforms them for purpose. In essence, mentorship is the divine bridge between potential and activation. It is where leaders are not only informed but formed.

In December of the year 2017, I joined a Toastmasters International club in Brooklyn, New York. I decided to sharpen my speaking skills and sought support beyond my usual circles. Shortly after I became a member, someone assigned me a mentor who was an experienced speaker. He made a commitment to walk with me as I grew in both confidence and craft. Over time, I formed a strong connection with another seasoned member who took on the role of mentor in a deeper and more personal way. As a protégé to these outstanding self-leaders, I became intentional about developing my skills, never taking their service for granted.

As I write this book today, my second continues to walk alongside me through challenges, opportunities, and the daily moments that shape who I am. She calls me two to three times weekly to check in and provide encouragement and that has been invaluable to my development and self-accountability. Her presence has deeply influenced my personal growth. That experience revealed the life-changing value of mentorship, and I encourage anyone seeking to grow to pursue it intentionally. Even so, I encourage you not to stop at mentorship alone. While guidance is essential, biblical mentorship rooted in truth, accountability, and generational legacy remains the higher calling.

Mentorship, when viewed through a Kingdom lens, is more than knowledge transfer, it is spiritual impartation. It is walking alongside someone with patience, wisdom, and accountability to help them grow into their God-ordained identity and assignment. It centers around cultivating character, clarifying calling, and cultivating courage. Today's Church and Christian marketplace need that same intentionality. It is not enough to produce talented people, we must nurture trustworthy ones. Mentorship is where trust is earned, faith is nurtured, and leadership becomes sustainable. It is not always formal. It does not always require a title. It simply requires presence, patience, and a heart to see others win.

> *It is not enough to produce talented people, we must nurture trustworthy ones.*

Dr. Myles Munroe demonstrated the ministry of mentorship with tremendous clarity. He mentored leaders across generations and continents. His mentorship model was not built on control, it was built on clarity and lives on today. He taught others how to discover their purpose, walk in integrity, and build systems that outlived them. He empowered leaders to rise in their own lanes, never threatening his platform with their success. That is the mark of true mentorship: it is never intimidated by the growth of others. In fact, it celebrates it.

Unfortunately, many leaders shy away from mentoring others because they fear being replaced, feel too busy, or believe they are not "qualified" to guide someone else. But mentorship does not require perfection. Every leader has something to pour and that is the starting point. Mentorship is not about having all the answers; it is about being willing to walk with someone as they discover them. Consider these questions: Who are you intentionally mentoring right now?

Who is walking with you, watching you, and learning not just from what you teach, but how you live?

There is an old African Proverb that says, "If you want to go fast, go alone. If you want to go far, go together." This principle is why mentorship matters. It is the difference between short-term influence and generational impact. To mentor well is to lead like Jesus. He poured His life into others, not so they would become dependent on Him, but so they would be empowered through Him. Mentorship is leadership in its most relational, personal, and enduring form. It is how Kingdom leaders reproduce themselves with intentionality and humility.

So let this be a call: do not just lead, develop. Do not just speak, walk with. Do not just build followers, form leaders. The legacy of leadership is not your résumé; it is your relational reach. And when you mentor with eternity in mind, the fruit will remain long after your season is done.

Finish the Race Well

As a leader, how you start is extremely important in laying a foundation. However, how you finish will largely determine the mark you leave in your wake. Many begin with passion, vision, and a clear sense of calling but somewhere along the way, distraction, disappointment, compromise, or fatigue cause some to fall short of the finish line. In contrast, those who finish well leave a lasting imprint, not because they were perfect, but because they were faithful. 2 Timothy 4:7–8 is the anthem of every leader who longs to finish strong where Paul said, "I have fought a good fight, I have finished my course, I have kept the faith: Henceforth there is laid up for me a crown of righteousness." It is important to note that by finishing well I am not suggesting that one needs to be perfect.

However, a leader must exercise persistence and purposeful leadership to finish well because leadership is a calling and should not be taken for granted. Dr. Henrietta C. Mears wrote about Paul in What the Bible is All About that, "many were leaving him under the stress of persecution."53 However, Paul noted that the Lord remained at his side and strengthened him so that he could still be used as a conduit to proclaim the message. (2 Timothy 4:17). It is clear that the secret of Paul's success was the ever-present Holy Spirit, the "Parakletos" who walked alongside him. Paul was by himself as far as human assistance was concerned, but the Lord was with him, and He will be with us also if we remain faithful in carrying out our work. Dr. Henrietta C. Mears who was an educator and spiritual mother to generations of Christian leaders, remained faithful to discipleship until her passing, impacting ministries long after her time. She also finished well from a general assessment of her walk and work.

Since leadership is a divine calling requiring individuals to lead by example by serving others generously, it does not retire with age or fade with titles. It continues until your final breath. The Apostle Paul clearly understood this as he saw his life as a race to be finished and a faith to be kept. These verses in 2 Timothy represent Paul's powerful declaration of a life well-lived in faithful service to Christ.

> *Charisma can carry you for a while, but only character will carry you to the end.*

Contextually, The Apostle Paul is writing to Timothy near the end of his life, reflecting on his ministry and anticipating his eternal reward. The very first part of his utterance reflects spiritual warfare endured with courage and shows he fulfilled his God-given assignment with perseverance. The last phrase emphasizes staunch loyalty to the gospel despite many adversities. This verse encapsulates the mark of true Christian leadership which embodies endurance, obedience, and faithfulness to the end. Paul knew his divine assignment and understood when it was fulfilled.

In Scripture and in life, we see leaders who begin with fire but fizzle before they finish and this, I believe is the epitome of failure in carrying out their mandate to the end like Paul did. For instance, in 2 Timothy 4:10, we meet Demas who was once a co-laborer with Paul, but deserted the faith because he loved the present world. He started out well but got distracted and moved away from his convictions. His story warns us that charisma can carry you for a while, but only character will carry you to the end.

Ultimately, fading in the final lap is truly a travesty. To finish the race well is the true crown of Christian leadership. It is the mark of a life lived in step with the Spirit, surrendered to the Savior, and committed to the mission. May your leadership be marked not only by powerful moments, but by a faithful finish. Let the cry of your heart be Paul's words, "none of these things move me...so that I might finish my course with joy, and the ministry, which I have received of the Lord Jesus, to testify the gospel of the grace of God" (Acts 20:24). Your cry should be, "no distraction, no discouragement, and no desire for comfort will stop me from fulfilling the ministry I have received and that is to boldly testify of God's grace."

EPILOGUE

This study was a powerful tool of illumination, deepening my understanding of leadership in general, and church leadership in particular. It changed me in a way that caused me to become more intentional in my leadership life and journey. It solidified the rediscovery that everything starts with seeking God first (Matthew 6:33). When I began, I thought I was simply writing about Christian leadership, its principles, practices, and pitfalls. However, somewhere along the way, I realized the purpose of the assignment transcended any impact it was meant to have on just me. It represented a deep dive into an honest assessment of my own way of leading others. God used this process to refine, convict, and gently realign my heart with His original design for leadership.

Here we are presented with the sobering truth that leadership in the Kingdom is not about control, visibility, or titles, the way it often is in the world. It is represented by sacrifice, service to others, and a willingness to persevere even when no one else is there to support you. David's story in 2 Samuel 24 still grips me. He stood in the gap, asking God to place the consequence of his failure on himself instead of the people he led. That level of humility and accountability allowed me to see that with intentionality, we can show up as responsible leaders even if the cost is high. David's response shows us that true leaders do not shield themselves from the cost, they absorb it.

We must accept that leadership is not a badge of honor as we perceive in today's society, instead, it is often a burden, and a holy one at that. It entails prayerful, private, persistent work. The kind of thing that happens in the margins when no one is watching. This is the kind of leadership Jesus modeled, and it is the only kind we should desire to emulate. Throughout the study, I was pressed to confront the unhealthy rhythms that creep into leadership when we idolize productivity and confuse exhaustion for effectiveness. I had to admit that balance is a lifeline, and it is important to make space for it. Jesus Himself modeled rhythms of rest, withdrawal, and reset. And if He did it, who are we to lead any other way?

This study offers readers a fresh perspective on the power of nurturing. Many come into leadership believing it is mainly concerned with results, decisiveness, and having the right answers. However, true leadership encompasses creating space for others to find theirs. One of the most striking revelations comes through Apostle Paul's tenderness in 1 Thessalonians. His example shows that leadership is not just about being strong. It is also about knowing when to be soft. Readers come to see that leaders are not commanders barking orders but gardeners. They water, they wait and most of all, they trust the process of growth in others.

We also see a reframing of the role of prayer in leadership as more than a mere add-on. Without prayer, leaders wind up performing rather than leading. They become edgy, reactive, and eventually exhausted. But with prayer, leadership flows from a place of spiritual clarity and authority. A key takeaway for any reader is this: **a prayerless leader is a powerless one.** Along the way, this study confronts some hard but necessary truths. We come to appreciate that the temptations are real; the pull to please people, the pressure to perform, and the subtle drift into burnout. These traps have taken many leaders out of position. Readers can clearly recognize these pitfalls early and walk with greater insight. Most of all, this study shifts the conversation on legacy which culminates with the need to prioritize finishing well. Readers who take this journey seriously will not only lead better, but they will also live better. They will learn to lead like Jesus.

My prayer is that what I have learned will not stop with me. Knowledge, when kept to oneself, remains limited in its reach, but when shared, it multiplies. I want to multiply what has been deposited into my life by intentionally investing in others. That means equipping leaders with truth, empowering them through wisdom, and encouraging them to pursue their calling with boldness and humility. I long to see a generation of servant-hearted leaders rise up, leaders who lead with conviction, uncompromised character, and Christ-like compassion. Leaders who are not driven by applause or ambition, but by assignment.

As you close the final pages of this book, may you recognize that leadership is not reserved for the few, but entrusted to the faithful. I pray you will no longer shrink back in fear, nor remain stuck in cycles of self-doubt, but will rise into the fullness of who God created you to be. May what you have read stir you to reflect, to realign, and most of all, to respond. Not someday. But now. Because the world is not waiting for more titles. It is waiting for more transformation. And that begins with you.

APPENDICES:

MANIFESTING YOUR INHERENT LEADERSHIP GREATNESS

"Leadership is not measured by how many follow you, but by how many rise because you served them well."

—Shauna-kaye Brown

THE 'SEEK' FRAMEWORK

The Purpose-driven Leader's Pathway to Encounter God Personally

"And ye shall seek me, and find me, when ye shall search for me with all your heart." Jeremiah 29:13

No matter your religious background or level of spiritual familiarity, one truth remains: God desires to be found. However, finding God is not a matter of religion, it is a matter of relationship so if your position is that, "I am not religious,' no need to worry. In Jeremiah 29:13, God extends a divine invitation to seek Him with all your heart. More than that, Matthew 6:33 urges us, "But seek ye first the kingdom of God, and his righteousness; and all these things shall be added unto you."

Do you realize this is the cornerstone of Christian living? Jesus is entreating us to prioritize God's kingdom above everything else? I am talking about His will, His standards, His way of doing things. When you do that, your needs (not greeds) fall into alignment. This isa call for us to prioritize our responsibilities and anchor them in the pursuit of God's purposes. Put simply, **Kingdom first, everything else follows.** Not hustle first. Not worry first. Not even ministry first, **Kingdom first.** Let *that* be the filter for your decisions, your relationships, your ambitions.

- Want peace? Seek the Kingdom.
- Need provision? Seek the Kingdom.
- Trying to make sense of your next move? Seek the Kingdom.

But how do we do that in a world filled with distractions, doubts, and demands? This is why I created The S.E.E.K. Framework which offers a practical and biblically sound pathway for anyone, believer or seeker, to begin their journey of spiritual pursuit and discovery.

SEEK

S – Silence the Noise

"Be still, and know that I am God..." (Psalm 46:10)

Create space in your day to quiet external distractions and internal clutter. God often speaks in the stillness, not in the noise. Stillness makes room for divine clarity.

Try this:

A. Sit in silence for 5-10 minutes.

B. Breathe deeply and pray, "Lord, quiet my heart so I can hear You." You must believe He can do this and them expect Him to.

E – Engage with the Word

"Thy word is a lamp unto my feet, and a light unto my path." (Psalm 119:105)

God speaks through His Word. You do not need to read large amounts, rather, focus on reading with intention.

Try this:

A. Read a short passage (for e.g., Psalm 23 or a chapter from the book of John).

B. Ask:

    a. What does this teach me about God?

    b. What is this revealing about me?

    c. How can I apply this truth today?

E – Express Honestly

"Pour out your heart before him: God is a refuge for us." (Psalm 62:80)

Talk to God with raw honesty. You do not have to sound spiritual. He already knows your heart. Vulnerability deepens connection.

Try this:

1. Write a journal entry or speak aloud: "God, I feel... I need... I am struggling with..."

2. End with: "Speak, Lord, I am listening."

K – Keep Pursuing Daily

"Draw nigh to God, and he will draw nigh to you." (James 4:8)

Spiritual growth is a journey, not an event. Even on quiet days, show up. God honors consistent pursuit.

Try this rhythm:

A. Morning: Read one verse and offer one sentence of prayer

B. Midday: Pause to express one moment of gratitude

C. Evening: Reflect on one way God may have shown up

Note

God is not hiding. But He does honor hunger. Your pursuit of Him is about being in His presence, you do not need to be perfect to get started. This framework is an invitation to experience the reality of God. If you seek Him sincerely, you will find Him, and in finding Him, you will begin to find yourself.

"But without faith it is impossible to please him: for he that cometh to God must believe that he is, and that he is a rewarder of them that diligently seek him." Hebrews 11:6.

THE 10 MOST ESSENTIAL ATTRIBUTES OF AN AUTHENTIC CHRISTIAN LEADER

A uthentic Christian leadership transcends performance and encapsulates presence and character It is who you are when no one is watching, and how you show up when everyone is. To lead with lasting impact, you must cultivate certain internal qualities that consistently align your heart with God's will and your actions with His purpose. These attributes practiced daily and integrated intentionally are the bedrock of spiritual authority, relational influence, and moral clarity. Every true and effective Christian leader carry these within them, not as perfection, but as a pattern of pursuit.

A. **God-Centeredness**: A true leader base their identity, decisions, and mission on a deep, abiding relationship with God.

B. **Servant's Heart**: Leadership begins with a willingness to serve others selflessly, just as Christ served His disciples.

C. **Emotional Wholeness**: Authentic leaders manage their emotions with maturity, allowing healing, not hurt, to shape how they lead.

D. **Moral Integrity**: Trustworthy leaders are consistent in character, doing what is right even when it is costly or unseen.

E. **Vision-Mindedness**: This is concerned with having a clear, God-given vision and inspiring others to move toward it with passion and purpose.

F. **Spiritual Sensitivity**: Discern and respond to the Holy Spirit's leading, and align your leadership with God's timing and direction.

G. **Faith-Fueled Boldness**: Instead of shrinking back in fear, take courageous steps entrenched in trust in God's promises.

H. **Teachability**: Humble leaders are always open to correction, growth, and learning, regardless of their position or experience.

I. **Compassionate Authority**: They lead with strength and clarity, yet always from a place of love, empathy, and respect for others.

J. **Steadfast Commitment**: Dependable leaders remain faithful through trials, opposition, and discouragement, anchored by their purpose.

K. **Wise Communication**: Ensure your words reflect discernment, grace, and truth, building up others and advancing the mission.

L. **Accountability Embrace**: They invite and submit to spiritual, relational, and organizational accountability to stay aligned and grounded.

These attributes are not traits you are simply born with, they are choices you make and attitudes you nurture over time. Reflect on each one regularly. Ask God to highlight where growth is needed in your life. Integrate them into your habits, relationships, leadership moments, and prayer life. As you walk in these, you will learn to lead authentically, in a way that honors God and transforms lives.

CHRISTIAN LEADERSHIP

NON-NEGOTIABLES

Ever the years, I have come to realize that each of us must stand for something, otherwise, we become unstable and inconsistent. Effective Christian leaders are distinguished not only by what they do but by what they refuse to compromise. To ensure you fall within this group, you must seek to cultivate habits, convictions, and disciplines that separate you from passive followers. These non-negotiables are not optional. They are the internal scaffolding of godly leadership. Therefore, if you are to truly manifest the leadership potential God placed within you, you must be willing to embrace and embody these values consistently. This

> *You must seek to cultivate habits, convictions, and disciplines that separate you from passive followers.*

list is not exhaustive, but it represents the kind of intentional living that marks a person who leads with purpose.

    A. Integrity

    B. Accountability

C. Prayer Life

D. Surrender

E. Compassion

F. Disciplined Living

G. Moral Courage

H. Radical Obedience

I. Honor

J. Active Faith

K. Accountable Relationships

L. Wisdom

M. Emotional Maturity

N. Servant Leadership

O. Spirit Sensitivity

P. Boldness

Q. Excellence Mindset

R. Continuous Learning

S. Inner Stillness

T. Relational Grace

U. Time Stewardship

V. Vision Clarity

W. Resilience Under Pressure

Let these words challenge your thinking. Reflect on each one and ask yourself: How does this show up in my life? What needs to shift? Write them somewhere visible such as in your journal or planner or on your mirror and revisit them daily. Use them as both a mirror and a map: a mirror to examine where you stand, and a map to guide where you are growing. Speak them over your life in prayer. Bring them into your workplace, your ministry, your relationships. Do not wait for a title, practice them now, because leadership is who you are, not just what you do. These non-negotiables will draw out the leader God already sees in you.

GUIDING BELIEVERS FROM SPIRITUAL GROWTH TO LEADERSHIP IMPACT

Spiritual growth reaches its fullest expression when a believer moves from being nurtured to nurturing others.

L eadership is a manifestation of maturity, service, and influence that has its foundation in the word of God. As you grow spiritually, you are not meant to remain passive recipients of truth but to become an active vessel of God's purpose in your spheres of influence. Encouraging leadership from within the faith community means nurturing character, building confidence in Christ, and modeling servant leadership. Whether you are personally seeking to step into leadership or feel called to help raise others up, these ten principles are foundational to ensuring that growth leads to godly impact.

A. Spiritual Maturity Precedes Ministry Leadership: Leadership begins with a solid foundation in the word, prayer, and spiritual disciplines. A leader must first be rooted before they can bear fruit.

B. Servanthood: Is the Model, Not Status: Jesus led by serving others. Kingdom leadership is marked by humility and a heart to meet the needs of others, not by titles or recognition.

C. Identity in Christ Fuels Confidence: When believers know who they are in Christ, they are empowered to lead without fear, pride, or comparison.

D. Vision: This is Birthed in Intimacy with God: Spiritual leaders do not manufacture vision, they receive it through prayer and relationship with the Holy Spirit.

E. Character Must Outweigh Charisma: Talent may open doors, but godly character sustains influence and credibility. Integrity, consistency, and accountability matter deeply.

F. Obedience: This is the Gateway to Influence: Small acts of faithful obedience often lead to much greater assignments. Leaders are forged in quiet yeses before they are entrusted with platforms.

G. Multiplication: This is the Goal, Not Just Impact: True leaders raise others. Leadership in the

Kingdom is generational and reproducible, it is not just about doing but about developing.

H. Community Sharpens Calling: Leaders experience the most growth in community where they are both supported and challenged. Isolation breeds distortion while connection cultivates clarity.

I. Grace Must Lead the Way: A leader rooted in grace leads others with patience, compassion, and understanding, especially through failure and growth.

J. Empowerment Requires Letting Go: To raise leaders, you must release control. Trusting others to lead, even imperfectly, is how leadership truly multiplies.

CLOSING REFLECTION

Manifest Your Greatness Now

You were never called to shrink,
nor to be buried under titles men assign.
Before the womb, God knew your name,
etched your purpose in divine design.

Not fashioned for the crowd's applause,
nor built to beg for man's esteem.
You were born to shift the atmosphere,
ignite the vision, stir the dream.

This greatness in you is not your own,
it flows from heaven's sacred breath.
It is not pride, it is His power,
placed in clay to conquer death.

Awaken now, do not delay,
the hour has come, the call is clear.
Do not rehearse what disqualifies,
faith walks forward, not in fear.

Lead with mercy, serve with fire,
build with hands both bold and clean.

Speak with wisdom, walk in justice,
guard the gate, but lead unseen.

Do not despise the quiet start,
nor curse the days that feel too small.
The stone rejected by the crowd
became the cornerstone of all.

Arise, release the oil within,
your voice, your heart, your sacred vow.
Not later, when you feel more ready,
but in obedience, manifest greatness now!

– With Love

Shauna-kaye

ENDNOTES

Introduction

[1] Robinson, Dr. Demetrius. *Keys to the Kingdom, Volume 1.* (Self-Published-Demetrius, 2017) p.51.

[2] Schuller, Robert H. *Tough Times Never Last, But Tough People Do.* (Thomas Nelson, Inc., Publishers, 1983), p. 29.

Chapter 1

[3] Munroe, Dr. Myles. *Becoming a Leader.* (Whitaker House, 2018), p.13.

[4] Blanchard, Ken, and Phil Hodges. *Lead Like Jesus.* (Thomas Nelson, 2008), p. 4.

[5] Nouwen, Henri J.M. *In the Name of Jesus.* (Crossroad Publishing Company, 1993), p.40.

[6] Idleman, Kylie. *The End of Me.* (David C. Cook, 2015), p.14.

[7] Franklin, Ryan. *The Christian Leader Blueprint.* (Blue Pioneer Publishing, 2023), p.88.

[8] MacArthur, John. *Called to Lead* (Thomas Nelson, Inc., Publishers, 2004), p. 51.

[9] Munroe, Dr. Myles. *The Spirit of Leadership* (Whitaker House, 2005), p. 220.

[10] Munroe, Dr. Myles. *Maximizing Your Potential* (Destiny Image Publishers, Inc., 1991), p.47.

[11] Warren, Rick. *The Purpose Driven Life* (Zondervan, 2012), p. 21.

[12] Strong, James LL.D., S.T.D. The Strongest Strong's Exhaustive Concordance of the Bible. (Zondervan, 2001), p.2053.

[13] Munroe, Dr. Myles. *The Principles and Power of Vision* (Whitaker House. 2003), p.61.

Chapter 2

[14] Whitney, Donald S. *Spiritual Disciplines for the Christian Life.* (Tyndale House Publishers Inc., 2014), p.83.

[15] Maxwell, John C. *The 21 Irrefutable Laws of Leadership.* (HarperCollins Leadership, 2022), p.9.

[16] Ibid, p.13.

[17] Maxwell, John C. *The 5 Levels of Leadership.* (Thomas Nelson, Inc., Publishers, 2011), p.71.

[18] MacArthur, John. *Called to Lead* (Thomas Nelson, Inc., Publishers, 2004), p. 21.

[19] Sanders, J. Oswald. *Spiritual Leadership.* (Moody Publishers, 2007), p. 75.

[20] Wilkes, C. Gene. *Jesus on Leadership.* (Tyndale House Publishers, 1998), p. 40.

[21] Munroe, Dr. Myles. *The Spirit of Leadership.* (Whitaker House, 2005), p.259.

Chapter 3

[22] Strong, James LL.D., S.T.D. The Strongest Strong's Exhaustive Concordance of the Bible. (Zondervan, 2001), p. 2437.

[23] Duvall, J. Scott and Hays, J. Daniels. *The Baker Illustrated Bible Background Commentary.* (Baker Publishing Group, 2020), p.462.

[24] Franklin, Ryan. *The Christian Leader Blueprint.* (Blue Pioneer Publishing, 2023), p.123.

[25] Warren, Rick, *The Purpose Driven Life* (Zondervan, 2012), p. 22.

[26] Maxwell, John C. *The 21 Irrefutable Laws of Leadership in the Bible.* (Thomas Nelson, Inc., Publishers, 2018), p.90.

[27] Munroe, Dr. Myles. *Becoming a Leader.* (Whitaker House, 2018), p.86.

Chapter 4

[28] Wilkes, C. Gene. *Jesus on Leadership.* (Tyndale House Publishers, 1998), p. 33.

[29] Sanders, J. Oswald. *Spiritual Leadership.* (Moody Publishers, 2007), p.25.

[30] Stewart, Robert. *Servant Leadership.* Robert Stewart (Self-published), 2022, p.1.

[31] Franklin, Ryan. *The Christian Leader Blueprint.* (Blue Pioneer Publishing, 2023), p.35.

[32] Stewart, Robert. *Servant Leadership.* Robert Stewart (Self-published), 2022, p.67.

[33] Munroe, Dr. Myles, *Maximizing Your Potential* (Destiny Image Publishers, Inc., 1991), p.98.

[34] Franklin, Ryan. *The Christian Leader Blueprint.* (Blue Pioneer Publishing, 2023), p. 222.

[35] Pue, Carson. *Mentoring Leaders* (Baker Books, 2005), p.14

[36] Maxwell, John C. *The Maxwell Leadership Bible.* (Thomas Nelson, Inc., Publishers, 2002), p.553.

[37] Munroe, Myles. *Understanding Your Potential.* (Destiny Image Publishers, Inc., 2008), p.88

Chapter 5

[38] Maxwell, John C. *Leader Shift.* (HarperCollins Leadership, 2019), p.7.

[39] Schuller, Robert H. *Tough Times Never Last, But Tough People Do.* (Thomas Nelson, Inc., Publishers, 1983), p. 64.

[40] Munroe, Dr. Myles, *The Principles and Power of Vision* (Whitaker House. 2003), p.17.

[41] Strong, James LL.D., S.T.D. The Strongest Strong's Exhaustive Concordance of the Bible. (Zondervan, 2001), p. 3994.

Chapter 6

[42] Zehentner, Markus and Schwinghammer, Claudia. *Breaking Free from Toxic Leadership.* (Zehentner Publishing, 2004). P. 41.

[43] Maxwell, John C. *Developing the Leader In You 2.0.* (HarperCollins Leadership, 2018), p. 185.

[44] Zehentner, Markus and Schwinghammer, Claudia. *Breaking Free from Toxic Leadership.* (Zehentner Publishing, 2004). P. 31.

[45] Pue, Carson. *Mentoring Leaders* (Baker Books, 2005), p.19.

[46] Zehentner, Markus and Schwinghammer, Claudia. *Breaking Free from Toxic Leadership.* (Zehentner Publishing, 2004). P. 191.

[47] Warren, Rick, *The Purpose Driven Life* (Zondervan, 2012), p. 319.

[48] Ibid p. 330.

Chapter 7

[49] Franklin, Ryan. *The Christian Leader Blueprint.* (Blue Pioneer Publishing, 2023), p.221.

[50] Warren, Rick, *The Purpose Driven Life* (Zondervan, 2012), p. 11.

[51] Franklin, Ryan, *The Christian Leader Blueprint* (Blue Pioneer Publishing, 2023), p.222.

[52] Strong, James LL.D., S.T.D. The Strongest Strong's Exhaustive Concordance of the Bible. (Zondervan, 2001), p.2067.

[53] Mears, Dr. Henrietta C. *What the Bible is All About.* (Tyndale House Publishers, Inc., 2011), p. 577.

SOURCE MATERIAL

Blanchard, Ken, and Phil Hodges. *Lead Like Jesus:* Nashville: Thomas Nelson, 2008, 272 pp.

Duvall, J. Scott and Hays, J. Daniels. *The Baker Illustrated Bible Background Commentary.* Michigan: Baker Publishing Group, 2020, 1427 pp.

Franklin, Ryan. *The Christian Leader Blueprint.* Louisiana: Blue Pioneer Publishing, 2023, 288 pp.

Idleman, Kylie. *The End of Me.* Colorado: David C. Cook, 2015, 218 pp.

MacArthur, John. *Called to Lead.* Tennessee: Thomas Nelson, Inc., Publishers, 2004, 225 pp.

Mears, Dr. Henrietta C. *What the Bible is All About.* Illinois: Tyndale House Publishers, Inc., 2011, 820 pp.

Maxwell, John C. *Developing the Leader In You 2.0.* New York: HarperCollins Leadership, 2018, 237 pp.

Maxwell, John C. *Leader Shift.* New York: HarperCollins Leadership, 2019, 265 pp.

Maxwell, John C. *The Maxwell Leadership Bible.* Tennessee: Thomas Nelson, Inc., Publishers, 2002, 1539 pp.

Maxwell, John C. *The 5 Levels of Leadership.* Tennessee: Thomas Nelson, Inc., Publishers, 2011, 289 pp.

Maxwell, John C. *The 21 Irrefutable Laws of Leadership.* New York: HarperCollins Leadership, 2022, 313 pp.

Maxwell, John C. *The 21 Irrefutable Laws of Leadership in the Bible*. Tennessee: Thomas Nelson, Inc., Publishers, 2018, 233 pp.

Munroe, Dr. Myles. *Becoming a Leader*. Philadelphia: Whitaker House, 2018, 252 pp.

Munroe, Myles. *Maximizing Your Potential*. Philadelphia: Destiny Image Publishers, Inc., 1991, 250 pp.

Munroe, Dr. Myles. *The Principles and Power of Vision*. Philadelphia: Whitaker House, 2003, 236 pp.

Munroe, Dr. Myles. *The Spirit of Leadership*. Philadelphia: Whitaker House, 2005, 300 pp.

Munroe, Myles. *Understanding Your Potential*. Philadelphia: Destiny Image Publishers, Inc., 2008, 285 pp.

Nouwen, Henri J.M. *In the Name of Jesus*. New York: Crossroad Publishing Company, 1993, 81 pp.

Pue, Carson. *Mentoring Leaders*. Grand Rapids: Baker Books, 2005, 268 pp.

Robinson, Dr. Demetrius. *Keys to the Kingdom, Volume 1*. (Demetrius, 2017) 130 pp.

Sanders, J. Oswald. *Spiritual Leadership*. Chicago: Moody Publishers, 2007, 244 pp.

Schuller, Robert H. *Tough Times Never Last, Tough People Do*. Tennessee: Thomas Nelson, Inc., Publishers, 1983, 237 pp.

Stewart, Robert. *Servant Leadership*. Robert Stewart (Self-published), 2022, 105 pp.

Strong, James LL.D., S.T.D. *The Strongest Strong's Exhaustive Concordance of the Bible.* Michigan: Zondervan, 2001, 2076 pp. Barbour Publishing Inc.,

The KJV Study Bible. Ohio: Barbour Publishing Inc., 2011, 1408 pp.

Warren, Rick. *The Purpose Driven Life.* Michigan: Zondervan, 2012, 361 pp.

Whitney, Donald S. *Spiritual Disciplines for the Christian Life.* Colorado: Tyndale House Publishers Inc., 2014, 352 pp.

Wilkes, C. Gene. *Jesus on Leadership.* Illinois: Tyndale House Publishers: 1998, 224 pp.

Zehentner, Markus and Schwinghammer, Claudia. *Breaking Free from Toxic Leadership.* Zehentner Publishing, 2004, 332 pp.

ABOUT THE AUTHOR

Shauna-kaye Brown is your proverbial 'renaissance woman' whose work spans law, personal development, ministry, education, publishing, organizational leadership, and global empowerment. She is a certified John Maxwell Speaker, Coach, and Trainer, a Distinguished Toastmaster (DTM), an Attorney-at-Law, and the founder of Transform Nations Now LLC, a faith-based initiative focused on cultivating bold, visionary leadership rooted in Kingdom purpose.

Her academic credentials include bachelor's degrees in Law, Theology, International Relations and Political Science. She also has a master's in Theology. Shauna-kaye holds a Certificate in Women's Entrepreneurship from Cornell University. With over two decades of experience in personal development and leadership formation, Shauna-kaye has trained and mentored individuals across generational, cultural, and professional lines.

Her body of work includes:

- 2020 Vision Devotional
- The Strategic Goal Setting Handbook
- The Strategic Goal Setting Workbook
- Co-authored anthologies: Courageous World Catalysts and Waiting in the Pit 2
- The Self-Starter Journal Series
- Illustrated The Bridge Series, a neurodivergent-friendly children's book collection by Khemele Hutchinson
- Editor and publisher of the book of Poetry, "We are What Remains" by Orantez Brown

Shauna-kaye champions transformational thinking, Christ-centered leadership, and the unapologetic pursuit of God-ordained purpose.

www.ingramcontent.com/pod-product-compliance
Lightning Source LLC
Chambersburg PA
CBHW022120080426
42734CB00006B/198